Pope Francis

MORNING HOMILIES V

Pope Francis

MORNING HOMILIES V

In the Chapel of St. Martha's Guest House
December 2, 2014 – March 26, 2015

ORBIS BOOKS
Maryknoll, New York 10545

ORBIS BOOKS
Fathers and Brothers MARYKNOLL™

Library of Congress Cataloging in Publication

Francis, Pope, 1936-
    [Sermons. Selections. English]
    Pope Francis morning homilies : in the Chapel of St. Martha's guest house /vols.
      1 – 3 translated by Dinah Livingstone.
     5 volumes cm
     Contents: I. 22 March–6 July 2013 II. 2 September 2013–31 January 2014 III. 3 February–30 June 2014 IV. 7 July–27 November 2014 V. 2 December 2014–26 March 2015
       ISBN 978-1-62698-111-9 (v. 1 : pbk.); ISBN 978-1-62698-147-8 (v. 2 : pbk.); ISBN 978-1-62698-179-9 (v. 3 : pbk.); ISBN 978-1-62698-228-4 (v. 4 : pbk.); ISBN 978-1-62698-294-9 (v. 5 : pbk.)
    1. Catholic Church—Sermons. I. Title.
BX1756.F677S4713 2015
252'.02—dc23

Contents

Preface

Each morning Pope Francis begins his day by celebrating Mass in the chapel of Casa St. Martha's, the Vatican guest house where he has chosen to live. Those in attendance vary, including other residents and staff, curial officials, visiting dignitaries, foreign bishops, representatives of religious congregations, or others who contribute to the daily upkeep of the Vatican, such as postal workers, gardeners, and the waste collection staff. This volume of the pope's *Morning Homilies*, the fifth in an ongoing series, is again based on the accounts published each day in *L'Osservatore Romano*. Through these accounts it is possible for those not present to experience and enjoy the pope's lively manner of speaking and his capacity to engage his listeners and their daily lives.

We know what great significance Pope Francis attaches to preaching. In his apostolic exhortation *Evangelii Gaudium* he dedicated an entire chapter to the homily, *the touchstone for judging a pastor's closeness and ability to communicate to his people* (EG 125). There he provided numerous guidelines for effective preaching, noting that the homily *should be brief and avoid taking on the semblance of a speech or a lecture*; it should be positive, *not so much concerned with pointing out what shouldn't be done, but with suggesting what we can do better*; it should respect the original intent of the text. (*If a text was written to console, it should not be used to correct errors.*) It should avoid abstract truths and cold syllogisms and it should make effective use of imagery. (Here he reinforced his point by recalling the words of an old teacher, who taught him that a good homily should have an idea, a sentiment, an image.) Above all, he likens the homily to a conversation "between a mother and child": *Even if the homily at times may be somewhat tedious, if this maternal and ecclesial spirit is present, it will always bear fruit, just as the tedious counsels of a mother bear fruit, in due time, in the hearts of her children* (EG 140).

From his Morning Homilies at St. Martha's we can see how closely Pope Francis heeds his own advice. His homilies are certainly short and positive, filled with memorable images. They are marked throughout by his familiar themes: the importance of mercy and forgiveness, the role of Jesus as Savior, the dangers of a church closed in on itself, the gospel as a source of life and joy.

But what is mostly striking is the intimacy and spontaneity of these homilies. Here is not the voice of a pontiff addressing the cares of the world, the universal church, or even the church of Rome, but a pastor sharing the Word of God with his immediate flock. He directs the message as much to himself as anyone else, acknowledging the same challenges, seeking the same consolation and healing.

The homily, as Pope Francis has observed, can be an *intense and happy experience of the Spirit, a consoling encounter with God's word, a constant source of renewal and growth* (EG 135). May that happy experience become available to all who read this book!

—Robert Ellsberg

Pope Francis

MORNING HOMILIES V

IN THE CHAPEL OF ST. MARTHA'S GUEST HOUSE

Only the Humble Understand

Tuesday, December 2, 2014
Isaiah 11:1–10; Luke 10:21–24

The grandeur of the mystery of Jesus can be known only by humbling and abasing oneself like Jesus, who went so far as to be "marginalized" and who certainly did not present himself as "a general or a ruler." Thus, theologians who do not "do theology on their knees" might have a lot to say, but "can't understand a word." Thus, Francis proposed humility and meekness during Mass at St. Martha's Guest House on Tuesday morning. "The liturgical texts that the church offers us today bring us closer to the mystery of Jesus, to the mystery of his person," the pontiff noted. And in fact, he explained, the passage from the gospel of Luke (10:21–24) "says that Jesus exalted in the joy of the Holy Spirit and praised the Father." After all, "this is the interior life of Jesus: his relationship with the Father, the relationship of praise, in the Spirit, the very Holy Spirit who unites that relationship." This is "the mystery of the interiority of Jesus, what He felt."

Jesus "declares that those who see him see the Father," Francis continued. He says, to be precise: "yea, Father, for such was thy gracious will." And "no one knows who the Son is except the

Father, or who the Father is except the Son and anyone to whom the Son chooses to reveal him."

The Father, the pope emphasized, "is known only by Jesus: Jesus knows the Father." And therefore, "when Philip went to Jesus and said, show us the Father," the Lord answered him: "Philip, he who has seen me has seen the Father." In fact, "the union between them is great: he is the image of the Father; he is the closeness and the tenderness of the Father to us." And, "the Father draws close to us in Jesus." Francis then indicated that "in the farewell speech after the Last Supper," Jesus repeats several times: "Father, that they may all be one; even as thou, Father, art in me." And Jesus "promises the Holy Spirit, because it is the Holy Spirit who creates this unity, as he does between the Father and the Son." And "Jesus joyfully exalts in the Holy Spirit."

This leads toward the "mystery of Jesus," the pontiff explained. However, "this mystery does not remain just between them. It has been revealed to us." Thus, the Father "was revealed by Jesus: he makes the Father known to us; he introduces us to this interior life that he has." The pope then asked, who does Jesus reveal the Father to? "To whom does he give this grace?" Jesus himself gives the answer, as read in the gospel of Luke: "I thank thee, Father, Lord of heaven and earth, that thou hast hidden these things from the wise and understanding and revealed them to babes."

For this reason, "only those with the heart of babes are capable of receiving this revelation." Only those with a "humble, meek heart, which feels the need to pray, to open up to God, to feel poor" have this capacity. In a word, "only those who go forth with the first beatitude: the poor in spirit."

Of course, the pope acknowledged, "so many can learn science, even theology." However, "if they don't do this theology on their knees, humbly, that is, like babes, they can't understand a word." Perhaps "they may tell us many things, but they won't understand a word." For "only this poverty is capable of receiving the revelation that the Father gives through Jesus." What's more, "Jesus comes not as an army general," not as "a powerful ruler." He will instead sprout, "as a shoot," like in the first reading from the prophet Isaiah (11:1–10): "There shall come forth a shoot from the stump of Jesse." Thus, Pope Francis said, "he is a shoot, he is humble, he is meek, and he has come for the humble, for the meek, to bring salvation to the sick, to the poor, to the oppressed, as he himself says in the fourth chapter of Luke, when he is in the Synagogue in Nazareth." And Jesus has come "for the marginalized: he marginalized himself; he does not have a nonnegotiable value, being equal to God." Indeed, the pope indicated, "he humbled himself, he debased himself." He "became an outcast, he humiliated himself" in order to "give us the mystery of the Father and his own."

The pope remarked that "we cannot receive this revelation outside, outside the world into which Jesus brings it: in humility, debasing himself." We can never forget that "the Word was made flesh; he marginalized himself in order to bring salvation to the marginalized." And "when the great John the Baptist, in prison, did not understand how things were there with Jesus, because he was somewhat perplexed, he sent his disciples to ask: 'John asks you: is it you or must we wait for another?'" Jesus doesn't answer John's question. "I am the Son," he says instead. "Look, you have seen all of this; tell John what you have seen": in other words, that "lepers are healed, the poor receive the good news, and the outcast are found."

According to Francis, it is obvious that "the grandeur of the mystery of God is known only in the mystery of Jesus, and the mystery of Jesus is really a mystery of lowering oneself, abasing oneself, humiliating oneself, and bringing salvation to the poor, to those who are destroyed" by sickness, sins, and difficult situations.

"Outside of this framework, we cannot understand the mystery of Jesus," the pope emphasized. "We can't understand this anointing of the Holy Spirit which makes us rejoice, as we heard in the gospel, praising the Father, and which leads to bringing the Good News to the poor and the marginalized."

From this perspective, in the season of Advent, Francis encouraged us to pray and ask the Lord to lead us ever closer "to his mystery, and to do so on the path that he wants us to take: the path of humility, the path of meekness, the path of poverty, the path of feeling ourselves sinners." For this is how, the pope concluded, "He comes to save us, to free us."

FOUNDED ON ROCK

Thursday, December 4, 2014
ISAIAH 26:1–6; MATTHEW 7:21, 24–27

Francis warned in his homily on Thursday that "so many good people" give in to the temptation to be Christians "only in appearance," wearing "makeup" that washes away with the rain. He also spoke again of the witness of so many "Christians of substance," who build their life on the "rock of Jesus" and live every day with "hidden holiness."

In the day's readings, one a passage from the book of Isaiah (26:1–6) and another from the gospel of Matthew (7:21, 24–27), the church "speaks of Christian strength and weakness; of rock and sand," Pope Francis began. Indeed, "a Christian is strong when he not only declares himself Christian, but when he lives his life as a Christian, when he puts the Christian doctrine, the Word of God, the Commandments, the Beatitudes, into practice." The key point is "putting into practice."

However, the pope remarked, there are those who are "Christians only in appearance: people who make themselves up as Christians, but in the moment of truth they have only makeup."

And we all know what happens when a woman, all made up, gets caught in the rain without an umbrella: "it all comes off, appearances wind up on the ground." That makeup, Francis acknowledged, "is a temptation." Thus, it isn't enough to say, "I'm a Christian, Lord," in order to truly be one. Jesus himself says that it doesn't suffice to simply repeat, "Lord! Lord!" in order to enter his kingdom. We must do the Father's will and put his "Word into practice." This is the difference between "a Christian in life" and a Christian "in appearance" only.

After all, the pontiff explained, it's clear that "the Lord is needed." First of all, "a Christian in life is founded on rock." In fact, Paul clearly says so when "he speaks about the water from the rock in the desert: the rock was Christ, the rock is Christ." Therefore, the only thing that counts is "being founded on the person of Jesus, following Jesus, on the path of Jesus." Francis shared that he has so often met "not bad people" but people who are "good, but who are victims of this 'Christianity of appearances.'" They are people who say, "I'm from a very Catholic family," or "I'm a member of that association and also a benefactor of that other one." However, according to the pope, the real question to ask these people is: "Is your life founded on Jesus? Where is your hope? In this rock or in these appearances?"

This is the importance of "being founded on rock." After all, "we have seen so many Christians of appearances that wash away with the first temptation, that is, with the rain." Indeed, "when the rivers overflow, when the winds blow—life's temptations and trials—a Christian of appearances falls, because there is no substance there, there is no rock, there is no Christ." On the other hand, however, "we have so many saints" among the people of God, Pope Francis stated, who are "not necessarily canonized, but saints! So many men and women who lead their lives in Christ, who put the Commandments into practice, who put Jesus' love into practice. So many!"

The pope recalled their testimony. "Let's consider the smallest: the sick who offer their suffering for the church, for others." And then, "let's consider the many lonely elderly people who pray and offer. Let's consider the many mothers and fathers" who work so hard for "their family, their children's education, daily work, problems, always with hope in Jesus" and "they don't strut about, but rather they do what they can."

Truly, Francis repeated, "there are saints in everyday life." He then spoke of "the many priests" who stay behind the scenes "but who work with such love in their parishes: catechesis for the children, care for the elderly and the sick, preparation for newlyweds. And every day it's the same, the same, the same. They don't tire because the rock is their foundation." Only those who live in "Jesus: this is what gives holiness to the church; this is what gives hope." This is why, the pope continued, "we have to take great care of the hidden holiness that there is in the church, that of Christians not of appearances but founded on rock, on Jesus." Look to those "Christians who follow Jesus' advice at the Last Supper: 'Abide in me.'" Yes, to the "Christians who abide in Christ," because, certainly, we are all sinners, but when "any of these Christians commit a grave sin" they repent, they ask forgiveness; this is great." It means having "the capacity to ask for forgiveness; not confusing sin with virtue; knowing well where virtue is and where sin is." We also understand from this that these Christians are "founded on rock, and the rock is Christ: they follow the path of Jesus, they follow him."

In the first reading, the pontiff explained, Isaiah "speaks of a strong city that has salvation, that follows God, that is righteous: a strong people. The city is a people. A strong people. Their will is steadfast and God assures them of peace: peace for those who trust in him." He then added, "Trust in the Lord forever, for the Lord God is an everlasting rock. For he has brought low the inhabitants of the height." In other words, Francis said, "the proud, the vain, the Christians of appearances will be brought down, humiliated." Isaiah has more to say about the "lofty city": that God "lays it low, lays it low to the ground, casts it to the dust." And this is precisely the way "the Christians of appearances end up," Pope Francis said, conjuring up the image from Isaiah: on one hand "the ruins of a city" and then "the other city, the other house, solid, robust because it's founded on stone."

The passage from Isaiah led Francis to another reflection. "It made me think of the last two verses of the first reading," referring to "this city that has fallen, this vain city, this city that wasn't founded on the rock of Christ." In fact, we read that "The foot tramples it, the feet of the poor, the steps of the needy." This expression, he said, "smells of punishment." Yes, "it seems like punishment," but "it isn't punishment."

Something similar is also said "in the song of Our Lady: 'he has put down the mighty from their thrones, he has humiliated the proud.'" Moreover, Pope Francis said, "the poor will be those who triumph, the poor in spirit, those who feel themselves nothing before God, the humble" who "bring forth salvation, but putting the word of the Lord into practice." However, Francis repeated, "all the rest is appearance: today we are, tomorrow we won't be." The pope then made reference to St. Bernard: "Consider, man, that you will be the food of worms." Because one day "we will all be eaten by worms"; unless "we have this rock, we will end up trampled."

Precisely in this season of Advent, "let us ask the Lord that we may be firmly founded on the rock that is him. He is our hope," the pope concluded. It's true, "we are all sinners, we are all weak, but if we place our hope in him we can all carry on." And this "is Christian joy: to know that in him there is hope, there is forgiveness, there is peace, there is joy." This is why it makes no sense to "put our hope in things" that are here today but gone tomorrow.

Going Out to Give Life

Tuesday, December 9, 2014
Isaiah 40:1–11; Matthew 18:12–14

The pontiff began his homily Tuesday morning with the day's first reading from the book of Isaiah (40:1–11), in which the prophet proclaims God's comfort to Israel. This prophetic promise passes through all history to reach us today. But when is it fulfilled in the church?

Pope Francis recalled that, as "a person is comforted when he feels the Lord's mercy and forgiveness, the church celebrates; she is happy to go out of herself." The joy of the church is to "give birth," and to "come out of herself in order to give life." In other words, the joy of the church is to "go out in search of those sheep who are lost," and to witness to "that very tenderness of the shepherd, the tenderness of the mother."

In recalling the words from the gospel of Matthew (18:12–14), the pope highlighted the impetus that drives the shepherd "who goes out," who "goes to look for" the lost and missing sheep. Yet, this zealous shepherd "can keep count like a prudent businessman." He loses one of ninety-nine, but his balance sheet still shows plenty of assets. However, Francis indicated, he "has the heart of a shepherd; he goes out to search" and, when he finds that one, "he celebrates, he is joyful."

"The joy of going out in search of faraway brothers and sisters" is born in the same manner. "This is the joy of the church." It is precisely in this way that the church "becomes mother, becomes fruitful." On the contrary, the pontiff admonished, when the church doesn't do this, "she stands still inside, she is closed within herself," even though "she might be well organized." And in this manner she becomes "a discouraged, anxious, sad church, a church who is more spinster than mother, and this church isn't useful"; such a church is no more than a museum.

The end of the passage from Isaiah returns to the image of a shepherd who "will gather the lambs in his arms, he will carry them in his bosom, and gently lead those that are with young." This is "the joy of the church: going out of herself and becoming fruitful," as in the time of Israel, when Isaiah proclaimed to the people those words of comfort offered by the Lord. Thus, in re-reading this passage the church opens herself to joy. She receives strength. Because the people are in "need of comfort." The same presence of the Lord "comforts, always comforts, either firmly or mildly, but it always comforts." Indeed, the pope stated, wherever the Lord is, "there is comfort and peace." Even in tribulations, he added, "peace is there," the peace "that is the presence of the Lord who comforts."

Unfortunately, men tend to run away from consolation. "We have mistrust, we are more comfortable in our things, and also more comfortable in our shortcomings, in our sins." It is here that man feels more at ease rather than "when the Spirit comes and comfort comes." This leads us to a condition beyond our control: the state of "abandonment in the Lord's comfort." It is in this situation that peace and joy arrive, as recalled in this beautiful expression of Hezekiah: "'unto peace he hath changed my bitterness,' for the Lord went there in order to comfort." It is also recited in the "psalm of the prisoners in Jerusalem, in Babylon: 'When the Lord restored the fortunes of Zion, we were like those who dream'—they didn't believe it!—'our mouth was filled with laughter, and our tongue with shouts of joy.'"

Indeed, when "the comfort of the Lord" arrives, "it disturbs us. It's he, not we, who commands. And the strongest comfort is that of mercy and of forgiveness," as Isaiah proclaims: "Cry to her that her warfare is ended, that her iniquity is pardoned, that she has received from the Lord's hand double for all her sins." From this point came the pope's call for reflection on how God's generosity cannot be transcended. "You have sinned one hundred times, partake two hundred times of joy: this is how God's mercy is when he comes to comfort," Francis explained.

Nevertheless, man tries to back away, because "this gives us some fear, a bit of mistrust: 'It's too much, Lord!'" In order to render understandable the infinite quality of God's mercy, the pontiff returned to the words of the prophet Ezekiel. In chapter 16, following "the list of so many sins of the people, so very many, he says at the end: 'But I will not abandon you; I will give you more, this will be my punishment: consolation and forgiveness.'" He is truly like this, "our God, the God who comforts in mercy and in forgiveness." This is why it's good to repeat: "Let yourselves be comforted by the Lord; he alone can comfort us."

Francis added that we so often "'hire out' small consolations," but these consolations "are useless; they may help but they aren't useful." In fact, what's useful to us is only what "comes from the Lord, with his forgiveness and our humility. When the heart humbles itself, that comfort comes" and we can be carried forth "by this joy, this peace."

The pontiff concluded with an invocation to the Lord, that "he grant us the grace to work, to be Christians" who are "joyful in the fruitfulness of mother church," and that he save us from the danger of "falling into the attitude of these sad, impatient, mistrustful, anxious Christians" who, in the church, have all that is perfect, yet bear no fruit. The pope asked God to console us with "the comfort of a mother church who goes out of herself" and with "the comfort of Jesus' tenderness and his mercy in the forgiveness of our sins."

God's Lullaby

Thursday, December 11, 2014
Isaiah 41:13–20; Matthew 11:11–15

God, out of his love for us, is like a mother who tenderly sings us lullabies and isn't afraid to even act "foolish." Francis thus called attention to the "temptation to commodify grace," affirming that "if we had the courage to open our heart to God's tenderness, how much spiritual freedom we would have!" To have this experience, the pope recommended we open the Bible and read the passage from the prophet Isaiah read during Mass at St. Martha's on Thursday: chapter 41, verses 13–20.

"The prophet Isaiah speaks of salvation, of how God saves his people, and returns to that image, to that reality that is precisely God's closeness to his people," the pontiff began. After all, "God saves by drawing near; he doesn't save from a distance. He draws near and walks with his people." This is the salvation of God, Pope Francis explained. Similarly, "in the book of Deuteronomy, he said clearly to the people: 'Tell me, what nation has a God as near to it as you?' None!"

Thus, "it's precisely God's nearness to those his people that makes salvation." It is a "nearness that advances, progresses up to taking on our humanity." And "in this verse there is something that might perhaps make us smile a bit, but it's wonderful," Francis explained. His nearness is so great "that God appears here as a mother, like a mother chatting with her child: a mother when she sings a lullaby to her child, using a childlike voice and making herself a little like the child and speaking with a childlike tone, to the point of acting foolish." The scripture reads in part: "Fear not, you worm Jacob." And how often does a mother say such things to a child while caressing him? The scripture continues: "Behold, I will make of you a threshing sledge, new . . ." In other words, Pope Francis said, "I'll make you big . . . !" And like this, the mother "caresses him, and brings him closer to her."

And God does this too. This is God's tenderness. "He is so close to us that he expresses himself with this tenderness, the tenderness of a mother." It's the same "even when the child doesn't want his mother and moves away, cries," as Jesus, seeing Jerusalem from the mountain, "cried, because his people had distanced themselves." God, however, "appears with a mother's approach: closeness."

Francis affirmed that "this is the grace of God." Indeed, he said, "when we speak of grace, we are speaking of this nearness." In other words, "when one says: I am in a state of grace, I am close to the Lord or I allow the Lord to draw near me, that is grace!" However, "oftentimes, in order to be certain, we want to control this grace, as if a child were to say to his mother: be good, be quiet now, I know you love me." And "the mother continues to say those things, which are funny, but it's love, the love that is always expressed this way." Does the child make his mother stop? "No! He lets himself be loved, because he's a child. Similarly, when Jesus speaks of the kingdom of heaven, he is like a child allowing himself to be loved by God." And "this is grace!"

Francis then highlighted that in history and also in life, we often "have the temptation to commodify grace," meaning to change "this grace which is the closeness, the nearness of God's heart" into "a commodity or something controllable." Because "we want to control grace." Therefore, "when we speak of grace, we are tempted to say: 'I have so much grace, yes, I am in grace!' What does that mean, that you are close to the Lord? 'No, I also have a clean soul, I'm in grace!'" What happens, though, is that "this most beautiful truth of God's closeness slips into spiritual bookkeeping: 'No, I'll do this because this will give me 300 days of grace . . .'" With this type of reasoning, grace is reduced to "a commodity."

Historically, the pope explained, "God's closeness to his people was betrayed, through this selfish attitude of wanting to control this grace, to commodify it." Francis gave the examples of "the parties in the time of Jesus." He first drew on the example of the Pharisees, who believed that "grace lay precisely in making law, following law and when there was doubt, to make another in order to clarify that law." But in so doing, "they ended up with three hundred, four hundred commandments." However, "when a mother caresses her child, she doesn't do this: it's freely given." The Pharisees, on the contrary, took what God had freely given and "carved out a path of holiness that enslaved them." This is why "Jesus reproached them: 'You who place such a burden on the shoulders of the people . . . ,' too many laws!" As a result, they rendered "God's grace, this nearness, commodified."

Then there were the Sadducees, the pope continued, who believed that "the grace of God was to 'coexist politically, the people with the occupiers, and to make political pacts,'" arguing that "we're fine, the people are carrying on, let's go this way . . . This is a grace, we are in God's grace since we are able to go on . . ." But Jesus reproached them for this too.

There were also the Essenes, who "were good, truly exceptional, but they were so fearful, they took no risks and they went into the monastery to pray." And thus "that grace which leads forward, that nearness of God became closure as monks in a monastery, but not with the grace of God."

From their song, however, "the zealots thought that God's grace was precisely that war of liberation, the freedom fighters of Israel." This was "also another way of commodifying grace." However, the pope indicated, "God's grace is something else: it's nearness, it's tenderness." He then proposed a rule that's always useful: "if, in your relationship with the Lord, you don't feel that he loves you with tenderness," this means that "you are still missing something; you still don't understand what grace is, you still haven't received the grace that is this closeness."

Francis then shared one of his experiences in the field, recalling when, many years ago, a woman approached him and said: "Father, I have to ask a question because I don't know whether or not I have to make confession." He continued, recounting the woman's words: "My husband and I went to our friends' wedding and there was a Mass, and we said: Is it okay, this Mass, Saturday evening? Does it pass? Is it valid for Sunday? You know, Father, that the readings weren't Sunday's; they were for the wedding, and I don't know if this was valid or if I mortally sinned because I didn't go to another Mass on Sunday." In asking this question, Pope Francis recalled, "that woman was suffering." And so "I said to that woman: 'the Lord loves you so much: you went, you received communion, you were with Jesus . . . Yes, so be calm. The Lord is not a merchant, the Lord loves; he is near.'"

Francis then spoke of St. Paul, who "reacted forcibly against this spirituality of the law." The law read, "I'm righteous if I do this, this, this. If I don't do this, I'm not righteous." Instead, however, "you are righteous because God has come close to you, because God caresses you, because God says these beautiful things to you with tenderness: this is our justice, this nearness of God, this tenderness, this love." And "our God is so good" that he runs the "risk of seeming foolish to us." Indeed, the pope affirmed, "if we had the courage to open our heart to this tenderness of God, how much spiritual freedom we would have! How much!" He then concluded with some practical advice: "Today, if you have a little time at home, pick up the Bible: Isaiah, chapter 41, from verse 13 to 20, seven verses. Read it," he said, in order to enter more deeply into the experience of "this tenderness of God," of "this God who sings to each one of us a lullaby, like a mother."

Darkness of the Heart

Monday, December 15, 2014
Matthew 21:23–27

"I ask the Lord for the grace that our heart may be simple, bright with the truth he gives us, and this way we can be kind, forgiving, understanding with others, big-hearted with people, merciful." This was Pope Francis' concluding prayer at morning Mass on Monday. "Never condemn," he said. "If you want to condemn, condemn yourself. Never limp with both legs, as Elijah says, trying to take advantage of situations." On the contrary, we must ask "the Lord for grace, that he grant us this inner light, that he convince us that he alone is the rock," and not those things we treat as important. We must ask "that he accompany us on the way, that he expand our hearts so that we can relate to the problems of many people, and that he grant us the grace to feel ourselves as sinners."

The source of the Holy Father's remarks was the day's reading from the gospel according to Matthew (21:23–27), wherein Jesus takes issue with those who look at people's spontaneous faith with formalism and norms that are often unhelpful. The pontiff introduced his reflection by recalling that when Jesus entered Jerusalem on Palm Sunday and "the children sang 'Hosanna to the Son of David,'" some of the "doctors of the law wanted to silence them." But Jesus said: "They cannot be silenced; if they don't cry out, the rocks will cry out!" The Lord then "healed many people," and when he was hungry, he went to a fig tree that had no fruit, and he cursed it: "May no one ever eat fruit from you again!" Afterwards the tree withered away, and when his disciples noted this miracle, Jesus replied, "If you have faith, you will do the same and more!"

In essence, Francis said, Jesus "preached about faith. Then he returned to the temple, healed many people, many sick, and cast out those who were doing business, selling, changing money." And this is when, witnessing these things, "the chief priests, the doctors of the law took courage and approached him," asking: "By what authority are you doing these things? We are here and command in the temple." Thus, Jesus answered "with inner zeal, with great acuity," in order to reach "the heart of these people." These were people "who had an insecure heart, a heart which adapted somewhat to circumstances, a heart which, according to the moment, went to one side or the other."

It might be considered "a diplomatic heart," but to the pontiff this definition is inaccurate, "because diplomacy is a very noble profession, a profession which brings people together, a profession for making peace," whereas "these people weren't doing this." Theirs was instead "a hypocritical heart." To them, "the truth didn't matter." They pursued their own interests "according to how the wind was blowing." In other words, "they were weather vanes, all of them." They had "an inconsistent heart, and negotiated everything: inner freedom, faith, homeland. To them what mattered in situations was a good outcome; they were situationalists, men who adapted to the trends: 'the wind is coming from there, let's go there.'" This was their heart: they took advantage of situations.

What's described in the gospel scene, Pope Francis explained, is one of these situations where they tried to take advantage. "They saw a weakness at that moment" or perhaps they imagined it, and decided "this is the time," and thus came the question: "Where is your authority?" Evidently "they felt fairly strong." But once again, Jesus caught them off guard. He "didn't argue with them" but reassured them, saying "yes, yes, I will tell you, but first tell me this," and he asked them about John the Baptist. Thus Jesus answered a question with a question, "and this weakened them" to the point that his interlocutors "didn't know where to turn."

And here Pope Francis linked his discussion to the Collect prayer from the opening of Mass, which asked the Lord to "cast light on the darkness of our hearts." In effect, the people that the gospel spoke of "had such darkness in their heart." Of course, "they observed the law: on the Sabbath they didn't walk more than one hundred meters and they never went to the table without washing their hands and performing ablutions"; they were "very law-abiding, very firm in their ways." However, the pope urged, "this is true only in appearances. They were strong, but outwardly. They were cast in plaster. The heart was very weak; they didn't know what they believed in. And this is why their life was, the outward portion, completely regulated; but their heart went from one side to the other: a weak heart and flesh of plaster, strong, hard."

Jesus, on the contrary, "teaches us that Christians must have a strong, steadfast heart, which grows upon the rock that is Christ" and which moves with prudence. Indeed, the pontiff continued, "you don't negotiate with the heart, you don't negotiate with the rock. The rock is Christ, it isn't negotiated! This is the drama of the hypocrisy of these people. And Jesus never negotiated his heart as the Son of the Father, but he was open with people, looking for ways to help." The others, rather, said: "You can't do this; our discipline, our doctrine says that you can't do this." And they asked him, "Why are your disciples eating grain in the field and walking on the Sabbath? You can't do this." In other words, "they were rigid in their discipline" and believed "the discipline is not to be touched, it's sacred."

Francis then added a personal recollection, linked to his childhood, "when Pope Pius XII freed us from that very heavy cross of the Eucharistic fast. You couldn't even drink a drop of water"—not even while brushing your teeth. The bishop of Rome confided that "as a child, I went to confess that I had taken communion, because I believed that a drop of water had gone inside." Therefore, when Pope Pius XII "changed the discipline—'Ah, heresy!

He touched the discipline of the church!'—so many 'Pharisees' were scandalized." Because Pius XII did what Jesus had done: "he saw the needs of the people, 'the poor people, with such zeal!' These priests who were saying three Masses, the last one at one o'clock, after midday, fasting. And these Pharisees were like this—'our discipline'—rigid in the flesh, but as Jesus says, 'decayed in the heart,' weak until decayed. Darkness in the heart."

And here lies "the tragedy of these people" whom Jesus denounced: "Hypocrites, you go where the wind blows, to take advantage!" In fact, they "were always trying to benefit from something." Pope Francis warned that this can also happen in our life: "Sometimes, when I've seen a Christian man or woman like this, with a weak heart, not firm, not steadfast on the rock, and with so much outward rigidity, I have asked the Lord: throw down a banana peel in front of him, so he takes a good slip, is ashamed of being a sinner and thus encounters you, who are the savior." After all, "so many times a sin can shame us" and allow us to "encounter the Lord, who forgives us."

"The Bible says, 'the heart of man is a thing of mystery,'" the pontiff continued, "who can understand it?" And this is why, he concluded, we have asked today, "Lord, cast light on the darkness of our hearts, that our hearts may be steadfast in faith." Just like those of the simple people in the gospel scene: people who "didn't make a mistake, because the doctors of the law knew they couldn't say, 'No, John's baptism doesn't come from heaven!' because the people knew, they had that sense of faith, which came from heaven."

They Shall Be First

Tuesday, December 16, 2014
Zephaniah 3:1–2, 9–13; Matthew 21:28–32

The basic condition for walking the "path of salvation" is a "contrite heart," one that is capable of recognizing its own sins. Thus, the Lord's "judgment" will not be one to frighten, but to offer hope. For this reason, the two readings that Pope Francis reflected on during Mass at St. Martha's on Tuesday have the very "structure of a judgment."

The pope first referred to the passage from the book of the prophet Zephaniah (3:1–2, 9–13), which begins with a threat, "Woe to the city, rebellious and polluted," and then a judgment: "to the tyrannical city," the city that "hears no voice, accepts no correction. In the Lord she has not trusted, to her God she has not drawn near." Those people are sentenced: the "sentence" is expressed in the term "woe." For the others, there is instead a promise: "I will change and purify the lips of the peoples," the prophet writes. "From beyond the rivers of Ethiopia," those who pray to me "will bring me offerings. On that day you need not be ashamed of all your deeds, your rebellious actions against me."

Who was Zephaniah talking about? He was speaking about those who drew near "to the Lord because the Lord had forgiven," the pope explained. These people were "the saved ones"; the others were "the proud, who didn't hear the voice of the Lord, who didn't accept correction, didn't trust in the Lord."

To the penitent, who were capable of recognizing: "Yes, we are sinners," Francis highlighted, the Lord reserved forgiveness and addressed "this word, which is one of those hope-filled [words] of the Old Testament: 'I will leave as a remnant in your midst a people humble and lowly, who shall take refuge in the name of the Lord.'"

Here the pope identified "the three characteristics of the faithful people of God: humility, poverty, and trust in the Lord." And this is "the path of salvation." The others, however, "heard no voice, accepted no correction, and did not trust in the Lord," and therefore "they cannot receive salvation": they are "closed" to salvation, the Holy Father explained.

The same thing happens today. "When we see the holy people of God, who are humble, who have their treasure in the faith in the Lord, in the trust in the Lord; the humble, poor people who confide in the Lord," here we meet "the saved ones," for "this is the path" that the church must take.

A similar dynamic is found in the day's reading from the gospel of Matthew (21:28–32), in which Jesus also proposes "to the chief priests, to the elders of the people," to the entire "'network' of people who waged war," a "judgment" to reflect upon. He presented them the case of the two sons whom the father asks to go to work in the vineyard. One answers, "I won't go to the field. I don't want to." But then he goes. Meanwhile the other says, "Yes, sir," but then thinks: "The old man has no strength. I'll do what I want; he can't punish me." And therefore, "he doesn't go, he doesn't obey."

Jesus asks his interlocutors: "Which of the two did his father's will?" Was it "the first, the one who said 'no,'" the rebellious one who later "thought of his father" and decided to obey, or was it the second? At this point Jesus offers his judgment: "Amen, I say to you, tax collectors and prostitutes are entering the kingdom of God before you." They "will be the first." And he explains why: "'When John came to you in the way of righteousness, you did not believe him. You didn't listen to John: the baptism of penitence . . . The tax collectors and prostitutes, however, believed. You, on the contrary, saw these things but then you didn't repent a bit.'"

What "did these people do" to deserve this judgment? "They

didn't listen," the pope explained, "to the Lord's voice. They didn't accept correction, they didn't trust in the Lord." One could ask, "But Father, what a scandal that Jesus said this, that the tax collectors, who betrayed the homeland because they collected taxes to pay the Romans." Will they really "go first to the kingdom of heaven"? And the same for "the prostitutes, who are throw-away women"? And finally, "Lord, have you gone mad? We are pure, we are Catholics, we partake in communion every day, we go to Mass." And yet, Francis underscored, they "will go first if your heart is not a contrite heart." And "if you have not listened to the Lord, haven't accepted correction, haven't trusted in him," then yours is not a contrite heart.

The Lord, the pontiff continued, doesn't want these "hypocrites who were scandalized" by what "Jesus said about the tax collectors and about the prostitutes, but then secretly went to them, whether to unleash their passions or to do business." They considered themselves "pure," but in reality, "the Lord doesn't want them."

Today's liturgy makes us think about this judgment, which is "a judgment that gives us hope when we look at our sins." Indeed, all of us, "we are sinners." Every one of us is well aware of our list of sins. However, Francis said, each one of us can say, "Lord, I offer you my sins, the only thing that we can offer you."

In order to better understand this, the pontiff recalled the "life of a saint who was very generous" and offered everything to the Lord: "The Lord asked him for something and he did it." The saint always listened and always followed the Lord's will. Yet the Lord once said to him, "You still haven't given me one thing." And he, "who was so good," answered: "But, Lord, what haven't I given you? I've given you my life, I work for the poor, I work for the catechesis, I work here, I work there . . ." The Lord pressed on: "You haven't given me one thing." And the saint repeated, "What, Lord?" And the Lord concluded, "Your sins."

And this was the lesson the pope wanted to highlight: that, when we are able to say, "Lord, these are my sins, they aren't this man's or that woman's . . . They're mine. You take them. This way I'll be saved." When we are able to do this, then "we will be that beautiful people—'the humble and poor people'—who trust in the name of the Lord."

We Are History

Thursday, December 18, 2014
Jeremiah 23:5–8; Matthew 1:18–24

In those "bad times" which inevitably arise in life, you must take on problems with courage, placing them in the hands of a God who makes history even through us, and corrects it even though we are unable to understand and we make mistakes. Pope Francis offered this suggestion during the Mass celebrated on Thursday, December 18, in the chapel of St. Martha's.

In yesterday's liturgy, we reflected on the genealogy of Jesus, the pontiff began. And with the morning's passage from the gospel of Matthew (1:18–24) this reflection concludes by telling us "that salvation is always in history; there is no salvation without history." Indeed, to arrive at the point we have reached today, he explained, "there has been a long history, a remarkably long history which, yesterday, the church symbolically chose to tell us in the reading of the genealogy of Jesus: God wanted to save us in history."

"Our salvation, the one God wanted for us, is not an aseptic, manufactured salvation," but "historical." And God, Francis affirmed, "made a journey in history with his people." The first reading, taken from the prophet Jeremiah (23:5–8), "says something beautiful about the phases of this history," the pope pointed out, rereading the words of the scripture: "the days are coming, says the Lord, when men shall no longer say, 'As the Lord lives who brought up the people of Israel out of the land of Egypt,' but 'As the Lord lives who brought up and led the descendants of the house of Israel out of the north country and out of all the countries where he had driven them.'"

This was "another step, another phase," Francis explained. Thus, "history is made step by step: God makes history," and "we too make history." And "when we make mistakes, God corrects history and leads us onward, onward, always walking with us." After all, if this isn't clear to us, "we will never understand Christmas, we'll never understand the mystery of the incarnation of the Word, never." For "it's all a history of walking," the pope commented, and obviously, it doesn't end with Christmas, because "now, the Lord is still saving us in history and walking with his people."

Here, then, is why we need "the sacraments, prayer, preaching, the first proclamation: in order to continue with this history." We also need "sins, for they aren't lacking in the history of Israel": in Jesus' own genealogy "there were many considerable sinners." Yet "Jesus went forward. God goes forward, despite our sins."

However, in this history "there are a few bad moments," Francis noted: "bad times, dark times, troublesome times" that bring problems "for the chosen ones, for those people whom God chooses to guide history, to help his people move forward." The pope recalled "Abraham, a calm ninety-year-old, with his wife: he had no son, but a beautiful family." However, "one day the Lord disturbed him" and commanded him to leave his land and set out on a journey." Abraham "was ninety years old" and that was definitely "a troublesome time" for him. But this is how it was for Moses too, "after he fled from Egypt: he married, and his father-in-law had a huge flock, and he shepherded that flock."

He was eighty years old and "he was thinking about his sons, about the inheritance he would leave them, about his wife." And then the Lord commanded him to return to Egypt to free his people. However, "that time was uncomfortable for him there, in the land of Midian. But the Lord bothers," and it's useless for Moses to ask, "But who am I to do this?"

So, Francis said, "the Lord bothers us in order to make history; he makes us go so many times on the path that we don't want." And he then recalled the story of Elijah: "The Lord impels him to kill all the false prophets of Baal and then, when the queen threatens him, he's afraid of a woman"; but "that man who killed four hundred prophets is afraid of a woman and could die of fear; he doesn't want to continue moving." It was truly "a bad moment" for him.

In the passage from the gospel of Matthew, the pontiff continued, "today we've read of another bad time in the history of salvation; there are so many of them." In the day's reading, the main character is "Joseph, betrothed: he really loves his bride-to-be, and she goes to help her cousin. And when she comes back the first signs of pregnancy can be seen." Joseph "suffers; he sees the women of the village gossiping at the market." And suffering, he says to himself about Mary: "This woman is good, I know her! She is a woman of God. What has she done to me? It isn't possible! But I have to accuse her and she will be stoned. They will say all sorts of things about her. But I can't lay this weight on her, about something I don't understand, because she isn't capable of infidelity."

Therefore, Joseph decides to "take the problem upon his shoulders and leave." And "this is what the 'gossipmongers' at the market will say: 'look, he left her with child, and then ran away so he wouldn't have to take responsibility.'" Joseph instead "prefers to look like a sinner, like a bad man, in order to avoid casting a shadow on his betrothed, whom he really loves," even though "he doesn't understand."

Abraham, Moses, Elijah, and Joseph, God's chosen ones, make history in their difficult times, by "taking the problem upon their shoulders, without understanding." The pope continued, returning to the story of Moses, "when, on the shore, he saw Pharaoh's army approaching: the army over there, the sea over here." He might have said: "What do I do? You misled me, Lord!" But then he takes the problem upon himself and says: "Either I go back and negotiate or fight and be defeated, or I kill myself and trust in the Lord." Facing these alternatives, Moses chooses the second and "the Lord makes history," through Moses and "in moments just like this, like a bottleneck," the pontiff described.

The pope then referred back to the story of another Joseph, "the son of Jacob: out of jealousy, his brothers wanted to kill him; then they sold him, he became a slave." And from this story the pope highlighted the suffering of Joseph, who also had "that problem with the administrator's wife, but he doesn't accuse the woman. He is a noble man: because it would destroy the poor administrator to know the woman was unfaithful." And so Joseph "shuts his mouth, takes the problem on his shoulders and goes to jail." But "the Lord goes to free him."

Returning the gospel, the pontiff again highlighted that "Joseph, in the worst time of his life, in the darkest moment, takes the problem upon himself," up to himself being accused "in the eyes of the others in order to cover his bride."

And, Pope Francis noted, "perhaps some psychoanalyst" would say this is "repressed anguish" trying to get out. But, he added, "they say what they want!" In reality Joseph took his bride with him, saying, "I don't understand a thing, but the Lord told me this, and this one is going to appear as my son!"

That is why "for God, making history with his people means walking and putting his chosen ones to the test." Indeed, "in general, his chosen ones went through dark, painful, bad times like these that we have seen"; but "in the end the Lord comes." The gospel, the pope recalled, tells us that he "sends the angel." And "this is—let's not say it's the end, because history continues—precisely the moment before: one history before Jesus' birth; then comes another history."

In consideration of these reflections, Francis recommended: "Let us always remember to say, with trust, even in the worst of times, even in moments of illness, when we realize that we have to ask for extreme unction because there is no way out, 'Lord, history did not begin with me nor will it end with me. You go on, I'm ready.'" And thus, we place ourselves "in the hands of the Lord."

This is the attitude of Abraham, Moses, Elijah, Joseph, and also of so many other chosen people of God: "God walks with us, God makes history, God puts us to the test, God saves us in the most difficult moments, because he is our Father." Indeed, "according to Paul, he's our dad." Francis ended his homily with a prayer "that the Lord enable us to understand this mystery of his journey with his people in history, of his testing his chosen ones who take upon themselves their suffering, the problems, even appearing as sinners—let's think of Jesus—in order to carry on with history."

THE TIME OF RE-CREATION

Friday, December 19, 2014
JUDGES 13:2–7, 24–25A; LUKE 1:5–25

In order to truly be "mother," the church must "let herself be startled by the newness of God," who through the Holy Spirit is able to "make all things new." Otherwise she risks becoming barren, afflicted by Pelagianism, selfishness, power, by the desire to "take over consciences" or becoming an "entrepreneur." Pope

Francis pointed out this temptation during the Mass at St. Martha's celebrated on Friday.

Francis' reflection was inspired by the day's readings: the births of Samson and John the Baptist announced by angels, as told in the book of Judges (13:2–7, 24–25a) and the gospel according to Luke (1:5–25). "Today, the word that the church makes us reflect on, prior to Christmas, the most important word today, is 'barren,'" the pontiff explained. The liturgy, in fact, "presents to us these two barren women who had no children; they weren't able to have any." The pope recalled that "in the people of Israel, barrenness was borne with difficulty: one could probably say that the inability to give life was considered almost a curse, because not having children prevented the fulfillment of the Lord's commandment to fill the earth with new lives."

Yet, he noted, "there are many barren women in the Bible, and always for important reasons." Starting with "Sarah, our mother: barren" but "the Lord performs a miracle." And "the mother of Samuel was barren too," and in this situation as well, "the Lord performs a miracle." And again, "the daughter of Jephthah went to the mountain bewailing her virginity, because she was not able to have children before she died."

Thus, Francis explained, "barrenness was a bad, bad thing." And today, the church "shows us this symbol of barrenness, just before the birth of Jesus, through a woman unable to have a child." This "is the sign of a humanity unable to take one more step: so many barren women were old, their wombs were no longer fertile." And "the church wants us to reflect on this barren humanity," on the humanity that "had reached the point where it could no longer go on." Recalling that "the law of Moses provided for the offspring of a dead man, because it was so important to have descendants, to give life," the pope remarked that "these barren women receive a miracle, they receive the grace of the Lord and they are able to conceive."

"From barrenness," the pontiff continued, "the Lord is capable of reopening a new lineage, a new life: this is today's message." Therefore, "when humanity is exhausted, it can no longer go onward, grace comes and the Son comes, and salvation comes." And in this way, "that exhausted creation makes way for the new creation, and thus we can call it a 're-creation.'"

Therefore, the truly "marvelous miracle of creation leaves room for an even more marvelous miracle: re-creation, as the prayer says today: 'You, Lord, who marvelously created the world, and more marvelously re-created it.'"

Thus, it is precisely "this 'second' creation when the earth is exhausted, and today's message: we await the 'master,' capable of re-creating all things, of making things new." And hence "we await the newness of God." This, after all, is Christmas: "the newness of God who remakes creation, all things, in a more marvelous way."

The pontiff then emphasized that "it's curious" that "in both texts, both that of Manoah's wife and that of Elizabeth, in order to explain how he will do this, how this will come about, the Holy Spirit is spoken of: 'the Spirit of the Lord stirred him,' it says." And "this 're-creation' is possible only with the Spirit of God." What then is the message? "Let us open ourselves to the Spirit of God. We can't do it alone. It is he who is able to do things."

The issue of barrenness, the pope said, "also makes me think of our mother church, of the many kinds of barrenness that afflict our mother church when, due to the importance of hope in the commandments, that Pelagianism that we all carry in our bones, she becomes barren: she believes she is able to give birth," but can't. Instead, "the church is a mother and becomes a mother only when she opens herself to the newness of God, to the power of the Spirit." It is "when she says to herself, 'I do everything, but I'm done, I can't give anymore,'" and then the Spirit comes.

Francis then asked to pray "for our mother church, for so much barrenness in the people of God: the barrenness of selfishness, of power." For "the church is barren when she believes she can do it all, that she can take over the consciences of the people, going the way of the Pharisees, of the Sadducees, on the path of hypocrisy." This is why we need to pray. And to do so in a way that this Christmas also renders "our church open to the gift of God," able to let herself be "startled by the Holy Spirit": a church "which has children, a mother church."

However, the pope indicated, "I have thought so many times that the church, in some places, is more an entrepreneur than a mother." Therefore, he concluded, "looking at this history of the barrenness of the people of God, and the many stories in the history of the church that have made the church barren, let us ask the Lord, today, looking at the nativity scene, for the grace of fruitfulness for the church." The grace that "the church may be a mother, first of all, like Mary: a mother!"

May the Lord Change the Hearts
of the Cruel

The Holy Father celebrated the morning Mass at St. Martha's in suffrage for victims of the cruel terrorist attack in Paris

Thursday, January 8, 2015
1 John 4:7–10; Mark 6:34–44

The attack in Paris yesterday makes us think of so much cruelty, human cruelty; of so much terrorism, both of isolated acts of terrorism and state-sponsored terrorism. The cruelty that man is capable of! Let us pray at this Mass for the victims of this cruelty. So many! And let us also ask for the cruel ones that the Lord may change their hearts.

In these days, the pope noted in his homily, "the key word in the liturgy is 'manifestation': the Son of God manifests himself in the Feast of the Epiphany, to the Gentiles; in Baptism, when the Holy Spirit descends upon him; in the wedding at Cana, when he performs the miracle of changing water into wine."

Indeed, "these are the three signs that the liturgy brings in these days in order to speak to us about the manifestation of God: God makes himself known." But "the question is this: how can we know God?" And with this, Francis referred to the day's first reading (1 Jn 4:7–10), specifically, "the theme that the apostle John takes up in the first reading: knowledge of God." Thus, "what does it mean to know God? How can one know God?"

To these questions, the pope answered, "A first reply would be: one can know God through reason." But really, "can I know God through reason? Somewhat, yes." Indeed, "through my intellect, reasoning, looking at worldly things, one can begin to understand that there is a God, and the existence of God can be understood in some of God's personality traits." However, the pope stated, "this is insufficient for knowing God," insofar as "God is known totally in the encounter with him, and reason alone does not suffice for the encounter; something more is needed: reason helps you to reach a certain point, then he accompanies you onward."

In his letter, "John clearly states what God is: God is love." For this reason, "only on the path of love can you know God." Of course, the pope added, "reasonable love, accompanied by reason, but love." Perhaps one could ask at this point, "How can I love one whom I don't know?" The answer is clear: "Love those whom you have near." In fact, "this is the doctrine of two commandments: the most important one is to love God, for he is love." The second "is to love your neighbor; but to get to the first, we have to climb the steps of the second." In a word, Pope Francis explained, "through love of our neighbor, we come to know God, who is love," and "only by loving reasonably, but by loving, we can reach this love."

Francis then repeated the words that John wrote: "Beloved, let us love one another; for love is of God, and he who loves is born of God." But, the pontiff recalled, "you cannot love if God doesn't give the love, doesn't generate this love for you" because "he who loves knows God." On the contrary, St. John writes, "he who does not love does not know God; for God is love." The pope pointed out that this is not "soap opera love," but rather "sound, strong love," an "eternal love that manifests itself—these days the word is 'manifest'—in his Son who has come to save us." It is, therefore, a "concrete love, a love of works and not of words." It is here, then, that "it takes a lifetime to know God: a journey, a journey of love, of knowledge, of love for our neighbor, of love for those who hate us, of love for all."

Pope Francis then indicated that Jesus himself "gave us the example of love." And, indeed, "in this is love, not that we loved God, but that he loved us first and sent his Son to be the victim of expiation for our sins." This is why "we are able to contemplate the love of God in the person of Jesus." And "by doing what Jesus taught us about love for our neighbor, we reach—step by step— the love of God, knowledge of God who is love."

The pope pointed out that the apostle John, in his letter, "goes a little ahead" when he states that "in this is love" and "not that we loved God, but that he loved us first: God precedes us in love." In fact, Francis noted, "when I meet God in prayer, I feel that God loved me before I began to seek him." Yes, "he is always first, he waits for us, he calls us." And "when we arrive, he is there!"

In this regard, the pope referred to another passage from scripture (Jer 1:11–12) and said: "How beautiful were God's words to Jeremiah: 'Jeremiah, what do you see?'—'a rod of almond, Lord'—'You have seen well, for I am watching over my word to perform it.'" Francis explained that "the flower of the almond tree is the first to blossom in spring, the first." This signifies that "the Lord is there, watching over," and he is always "the first, like the almond tree, he loves us first." And we, too, the pope assured us, "will always have this surprise: when we draw near to God through works of charity, through prayer, in communion, in the word of God, we find that he is there, first, waiting for us; this is how he loves us." And just "like the flower of the almond tree, he is the first." Truly, Francis remarked, "that verse from Jeremiah tells us so much."

A similar proposal can be gleaned from the episode presented in today's reading from the gospel according to Mark (6:34–44), which first says that "Jesus had compassion on the crowd of people, it is the love of Jesus: he saw a large crowd, like sheep without a shepherd, confused." But today as well, Francis recalled, there are "so many confused people in our cities, in our countries: so many people."

When "Jesus saw these confused people he was moved. He began to teach them the doctrine, the matters of God, and the people heard him, listened to him very closely because the Lord was good at speaking; he spoke to the heart."

Then, Mark recounts in his gospel that, realizing that those 5,000 people hadn't eaten, Jesus asks his disciples to see to it. Thus, Christ "is first to go meet with the people." Perhaps on their part, "the disciples got somewhat upset, felt annoyed, and their response was harsh: 'shall we go and buy two hundred denarii worth of bread and give it to them to eat?'" Thus, "God's love was first; the disciples hadn't understood." But God's love is really like this: "He is always waiting for us, he always surprises us." It is "the Father, our Father who loves us so much, who is always ready to forgive us, always. And not once, but seventy times seven. Always!" Indeed, "like a Father full of love." Therefore, "in order to know this God who is love, we must climb the steps of love for our neighbor, by works of charity, by the acts of mercy that our Lord has taught us."

Francis concluded by praying "that the Lord, in these days in which the church makes us ponder the manifestation of God, grant us the grace to know him on the path of love."

HARDENED HEARTS

Friday, January 9, 2015
1 JOHN 4:11–18; MARK 6:45–52

A hardened heart is unable to comprehend even the greatest miracles. But "how does a heart become hardened?" Pope Francis asked during Mass at St. Martha's on Friday morning.

In the passage of the gospel according to Mark (6:45–52), we read that the disciples "did not understand about the loaves, but their hearts were hardened." Yet, Francis explained, "they were the apostles, the ones closest to Jesus. But they didn't understand." Even witnessing the miracle, even having "seen that those people—more than five thousand—had eaten of five loaves," they didn't comprehend. "Why? Because their hearts were hardened."

The pope said that many times in the gospel, Jesus "speaks of hardness of the heart," he rebukes "the stiff-necked people," he weeps over Jerusalem, "which doesn't understand who he is." The Lord is faced with this hardness: it is "such work" for Jesus "to make this heart more docile, to remove the hardness, to make it loving," Francis continued. And this work continues after the resurrection, with the disciples of Emmaus and many others.

However, the pontiff asked, "how does a heart become hardened? How is it possible that these people, who were always with

Jesus, every day, who heard him, saw him . . . their hearts hardened. But how can a heart become like this?"

The pope recounted: "Yesterday, I asked my secretary: Tell me, how does a heart become hardened? He helped me think a bit about this." Francis went on to indicate a series of circumstances that each person might face in his or her own personal experience.

First of all, Francis said, the heart "becomes hardened through painful experiences, through harsh experiences." This is the situation of those who "have lived a very painful experience and don't want to begin another adventure." This is just what happened to the disciples of Emmaus after the resurrection, and the pontiff set the scene: "'There is too much, too much commotion, so let's get away from here, because . . .'" Because what?—'Well, we were hoping this would be the Messiah. He wasn't there; I don't want to delude myself again, I don't want to create illusions!'"

This is a heart hardened by a "painful experience." The same thing happened to Thomas: "No, no, I don't believe it. Unless I place my finger there, I won't believe it." The disciples' hearts were hard "because they had suffered." And in this regard, Francis recalled a popular Argentine saying: "One who burns himself with milk will cry when he sees a cow." In other words, he explained, "that painful experience keeps us from opening our heart."

Another reason the heart becomes hardened is "becoming closed inside oneself: making a world within oneself." This happens when man is "closed inside himself, in his community or in his parish." It is a closing off which "can turn around many things," such as "pride, sufficiency, thinking that I'm better than others," or even "vanity." The pope noted, "There are 'mirror' men and women, who are closed within themselves to watch themselves, constantly"; they could be defined as "religious narcissists." They "have hard hearts because they are closed, they aren't open. And they try to protect themselves with these walls they build around themselves."

There is yet another reason that the heart becomes hardened: insecurity. It is experienced by those who think, "I don't feel secure and I am trying to hang on to something to be secure." This attitude is typical of people "who really stick to the letter of the law." This happens, the pontiff explained, "with the Pharisees, with the Sadducees, with the doctors of the law in the time of Jesus." They would have objected: "But the law says this, it says this up to here . . . ," and thus "they would make another commandment"; in the end, "the poor souls, they were leaning on three hundred–four hundred commandments and they felt secure."

In reality, Francis pointed out, all of them "were secure people, but as a man or woman in a prison cell is secure behind bars: it's a security without freedom." However, it is actually freedom that "Jesus came to bring us." St. Paul, for example, rebukes James and Peter "because they do not accept the freedom that Jesus has brought us."

Hence the response to the initial question: "How does a heart become hardened?" The heart, in fact, "when it hardens, is not free, and if it isn't free it's because it does not love." This concept is expressed in the day's first reading (1 Jn 4:11–18), in which the apostle John speaks of "perfect love" that "casts out fear." Indeed, "'there is no fear in love, but perfect love casts out fear. For fear has to do with punishment, and he who fears is not perfected in love.' He isn't free. He always fears that something painful or sad might happen," which could cause us to "go the wrong way in life or to risk eternal salvation." Instead, this is only imagined, simply because that heart doesn't love. The disciples' hearts, the pope explained, "were hardened because they still hadn't learned how to love."

Thus, here, we can ask, "Who teaches us how to love? Who frees us from this hardness?" The pope's answer: "the Holy Spirit alone" can do so. "You can take a thousand courses in catechesis, a thousand courses in spirituality, a thousand courses in yoga, Zen, and all these things. But all of this will never be able to give you the freedom of the Son." Only the Holy Spirit "moves your heart to say 'Father'"; he alone "is capable of casting out, of breaking, this hardness of the heart" and of making it "docile to the Lord. Docile to the freedom of love." It is no coincidence that the disciples' hearts were "hardened until the day of the ascension," when they said to the Lord: "Now the revolution will happen and the kingdom will come!" However, "they didn't understand a thing." In reality, "only when the Holy Spirit came did things change."

Therefore, the pontiff concluded, "let us ask the Lord for the grace to have a docile heart, that he save us from the slavery of a hardened heart" and "lead us to that beautiful freedom of perfect love, the freedom of the children of God, which the Holy Spirit alone can give."

He Who Intercedes on Our Behalf

Thursday, January 22, 2015
Hebrews 7:25; 8:6; Mark 3:1–12

Jesus saves and Jesus intercedes: these are the two key words to understanding the essential point that is most important for our life. This is the truth of faith that Pope Francis reaffirmed in the Mass at St. Martha's on Thursday morning.

Present at the celebration were representatives of Rome's Slovak community. Welcoming them at the beginning of Mass, the pontiff expressed closeness to the "courageous Slovak Church, which at this moment, at this time, is fighting to defend the family. Continue with courage!"

Meditating on the ministry of Jesus, the pope turned to the day's gospel passage (Mk 3:1–12), noting the repetition of the word "multitude." The passage tells us, he explained, that "the people of God find hope in Jesus because his way of acting, of teaching, touches the heart, reaches the heart because it has the power of the word of God." And that "the people feel this and see that promises are fulfilled in Jesus, that in Jesus there is hope."

After all, Francis added, the "people were rather bored with the way of teaching the faith by the doctors of the law of that time, who loaded them down with many commandments, many precepts, but did not reach the people's heart." This is why, "when they see and hear Jesus, his proposals, the Beatitudes, they feel something moving inside—it's the Holy Spirit that causes this—and they go to look for Jesus."

But Mark the evangelist, according to Francis, "wants to explain why so many people come to Jesus." The gospel tells us that "he speaks with authority; he doesn't speak like the scribes, the Pharisees, the doctors of the law." Then "Jesus heals people" who, in any case, are "in search of self-goodness." After all, the pontiff acknowledged, "we are never able to follow God with purity of intention from the start," as we are instead "partly for us, partly for God, and the path is for purifying this intention." Thus, "the people go, seeking God, but also seeking health, healing." And for this reason "they threw themselves at him, to touch him, so that power would come out and heal them."

"Jesus is like this," Francis explained. "And this is a moment which recurs in Jesus' life." However, "there is something more important behind this." In fact, what is truly "most important is not that Jesus heals," which is also "a sign of another healing." Nor that "Jesus utters words that reach the heart," even though "this helps us to go on God's path."

To better comprehend "what is most important in Jesus' ministry," Francis returned to the message of the first reading (Heb 7:25; 8:6), where he indicated two fundamental words: "Brothers, Christ 'is able for all time to save,' in a perfect way, 'those who draw near to God through him, since he always lives to make intercession for them.'" Thus, he said, "Jesus saves and Jesus intercedes. These are the two key words."

Yes, the pope repeated, "Jesus saves!" And "these healings, these words that reach the heart are the sign and the beginning of salvation." They are "the way to salvation for many who begin to go to hear Jesus or to ask for healing and then turn to him and feel salvation. See, then, Francis said, the more important thing is not that Jesus heals and teaches, but that he saves. For "he is the savior and we are saved through him." This is "more important" and it "is the strength of our faith."

The second key word is "intercede." Indeed, the pope recalled, "Jesus has gone to the Father and from there he still intercedes, every day, at all times for us." And "this is something current: Jesus before the Father, who offers his life, the redemption, showing the Father his wounds, the price of salvation." And like this, "every day Jesus intercedes." This is why "when we, for one reason or another," feel "a little down, let's remember that it is he who prays for us, intercedes for us continuously." However, he noted, "we often forget this." But Jesus did not "go to heaven, send us the Holy Spirit, end of story! No! Presently, every moment, Jesus intercedes."

In this regard, Francis suggested that we pray with these simple words: "'Lord Jesus, have mercy on me. Intercede for me.'" It's important, he continued, "to turn to the Lord asking for this intercession." The crucial point is what the author of the letter to the Hebrews writes, reminding us that we have "such a grand high priest, one who is seated at the right hand of the throne of the Majesty in heaven." This is "the crucial point: that there, we have an intercessor." And the pope said not to forget "that the Lord is the intercessor: the savior and the intercessor," adding that "it will do us good to remember this."

In conclusion, the pontiff continued, "the multitude seeks

Jesus," trailing "that scent of hope of the people of God who await the Messiah, and they try to find in him health, truth, salvation, for he is the savior and as savior he still today, at this moment, intercedes for us." Francis ended with the hope "that our Christian life may be ever more confident that we have been saved, that we have a savior, Jesus, at the right hand of the Father, who intercedes. May the Lord, the Holy Spirit, enable us to understand these things."

WHEN GOD FORGETS

Friday, January 23, 2015
HEBREWS 8:6–13; MARK 3:13–19

Confession is not a judgment nor is it like going to the dry cleaners remove the stain of sins. It is the encounter with a Father who always forgives, forgives all, forgets the faults of the past, and then even celebrates. And it is the embrace of God's reconciliation that the pope spoke about on Friday morning, during Mass at St. Martha's, where representatives of Rome's Filipino community were present. They gathered closely around him to relive the joy of the recent pastoral journey.

"God reconciled the world to himself in Christ and entrusted to us the message of reconciliation" (cf. 2 Cor 5:19). Francis chose this point of departure for his meditation. "It is beautiful, this work of God: to reconcile," the pope remarked, pointing out the task that God entrusts to us: "to make reconciliation, to always reconcile."

There is no doubt, he said, that "a Christian is a man or woman of reconciliation, not of division." After all, "the father of division is the devil." God himself gives "this example of reconciling the world, the people." He was referring to what we heard in the first reading from the letter to the Hebrews (8:6–13), particularly to "that most beautiful promise: 'I will establish a new covenant.'"

A question so decisive, said the bishop of Rome, that "covenant is mentioned five times in this passage." Indeed "it is God who reconciles, creating a new relationship with us, a new covenant." And "to do this he sends Jesus; the God who reconciles is the God who forgives."

The passage from the letter to the Hebrews, Francis continued, "ends with that beautiful promise: 'and I remember their sins no more.'" He is "the God who forgives; our God forgives, reconciles, establishes the new covenant and forgives." But "how does God forgive? First of all, God always forgives! He never tires of forgiving. It is we who tire of asking forgiveness. But he never tires of forgiving." Indeed, "when Peter asks Jesus, How often shall I forgive, seven times?" he received an eloquent reply: "not seven times, but seventy times seven" (cf. Mt 18:21–22). In other words, "always," because "this is how God forgives: always." Therefore, "if you have lived a life of many sins, many bad things, but at the end, contritely ask for forgiveness, he forgives you straightaway. He always forgives."

However, Pope Francis recognized, "we do not have this certainty in our heart and many times we are doubtful," wondering whether God will forgive. In reality, he recalled, "we need only repent and ask for forgiveness: nothing more! It costs us nothing! Christ paid for us and he always forgives."

Another important thing the pontiff wanted to reinforce is that not only does God "always forgive," but he also forgives "all: there is no sin that he would not forgive." Perhaps, the pope explained, someone could say: "I don't go to confession because I have done so many bad things, so many of those things for which I will not be forgiven . . ." However, "it isn't true," Francis emphasized, because "if you go contritely," then God "forgives all." And "many times he doesn't let you speak: you start asking for forgiveness and he makes you feel that joy of forgiveness before you have finished saying everything." It is just "as it happened with that son who, after squandering all the money of his inheritance with an immoral life," and then "he repented" and prepared a speech to present to his father. However, "when he arrived the father didn't let him speak, he embraced him: because he forgives all. He embraced him."

And then, "there is another thing God does when he forgives: he celebrates." And this, the pontiff indicated, "is not imagined; Jesus says it: 'There will be a feast in heaven when a sinner goes to the Father.'" Truly, "God celebrates." Thus, "when we feel our heart heavy with sins, we can say: let's go to the Lord to give him joy, so that he may forgive us and celebrate." God works in this way: "He always celebrates because he reconciles."

Continuing his meditation on the letter to the Hebrews, the pope proposed the final words again. They suggest, he explained, "something beautiful about the way God forgives: God forgets." Scripture also puts it in other words: "Your sins shall be cast into the sea, and though they are red like blood, they shall become white as a lamb" (cf. Mic 7:19; Is 1:18).

Hence, God forgets, and "if one of us goes to the Lord" and says, "Do you remember, in that year I did something bad?" He answers: "No, no, no. I don't remember." Because "once he forgives he no longer remembers, he forgets," while "so often, with others, we 'keep a record': this one did this, another one once did that . . ." But God doesn't do this: "He forgives and forgets." However, Francis asked himself, "if he forgets, who am I to remember the sins of others?" Thus, the Father "forgets, always forgives, forgives all, celebrates when he forgives, and he forgets, because he wants to reconcile, he wants to encounter us."

In the light of this reflection the pope recalled that "when one of us—a priest, a bishop—goes to confess, he must always think:

am I ready to forgive all? Am I always ready to forgive all? Am I ready to rejoice and celebrate? Am I ready to forget that person's sins?" Because, "if you aren't ready, it's better that you don't enter the confessional that day, that someone else go, because you don't have the heart of God to forgive." Indeed, "in confession, it's true, there's a judgment, because the priest judges," saying, "You've done harm here, you did . . ." However, the pope explained, "it is more than a judgment: it's an encounter, an encounter with the good God who always forgives, who forgives all, who knows how to celebrate when he forgives, and who forgets your sins when he forgives you." And "we priests need to have this attitude" of encounter. Otherwise, "so often confessions seem to be a practice, a formality," where everything appears "mechanical." But like this, the pontiff asked, where is "the encounter with the Lord who reconciles, embraces you and celebrates? This is our God," who is "so good."

The pontiff pointed out the importance of teaching children how to make a good confession, reminding them that "going to confession isn't like going to the dry cleaner to have a stain removed." Confession "is going to encounter the Father who reconciles, who forgives and who celebrates."

In conclusion Francis recommended that we "think of this covenant that the Lord makes each time that we ask for forgiveness." And also that we think "of our Father who always reconciles—God who reconciled the world to himself in Christ and entrusted to us the message of reconciliation"—in the hope that "the Lord may give us grace of being content today to have a Father who always forgives, who forgives all, who celebrates when he forgives and who forgets our history of sin!"

We Owe It All to Women

Monday, January 26, 2015
2 Timothy 1:1–8; Mark 3:22–30

There is no timidity or shame in being Christians, for faith is "a spirit of power and love and self-control." This was Pope Francis' teaching from the liturgical commemoration of Sts. Titus and Timothy, disciples of the apostle of the peoples.

Celebrating Mass at St. Martha's on Monday morning, the pontiff paused particularly on the first reading, taken from the second letter of Paul to Timothy (1:1–8). He emphasized that the Christian faith gives us "the power to live, when we rekindle this gift of God. It gives us love, it gives us charity," in order "to render the faith fruitful. And it gives us the spirit of self-control: that is, knowing that we are not able to do all that we want" since "on our journey we must go onward and look for the ways, the means to carry it forward."

At the beginning of the homily, the pope pointed out that Bishops Timothy and Titus are like sons to Paul, who "loves both of them very much." The apostle speaks of Timothy's "sincere faith" (2 Tim 1:5), in other words, "a noble faith." Moreover, according to Francis, the original text could be translated as a "faith without hypocrisy," a "faith in the true sense." Basically, "like a good wine which, after many years, is 'up front,' noble."

The pontiff then recalled that Paul also reveals the origin of Timothy's faith. He received it, in fact, from his grandmother Lois and from his mother, Eunice. Because, Pope Francis remarked, it is "the mothers, the grandmothers who pass down the faith."

On this point, Francis clarified that "it's one thing to pass down the faith and another thing to teach the truths of the faith." Indeed "faith is a gift. Faith cannot be studied. We study the truths of the faith in order to understand it better, but faith is never reached by studying. Faith is a gift of the Holy Spirit; it's a gift that goes beyond any preparation." Regarding this aspect the pope noted that Timothy was a young bishop, for in the first reading Paul says to him: "Let no one despise your youth" (1 Tim 4:12). It is likely "that someone, seeing how young he was," would scorn him, posing arguments such as: "This youngster who comes to command here . . ." But, Francis continued, "the Holy Spirit chose him." And thus, "this young bishop" hears Paul say, "Remember where your faith comes from, who gave it to you, the Holy Spirit, through your mother and grandmother."

Pope Francis then recalled "the beautiful work of mothers and grandmothers, the beautiful service of those women who act as mothers and the women in the family—she might even be a housekeeper, maybe an aunt—in passing on the faith."

Then returning to the sincerity of Timothy's faith praised by Paul, the pontiff noted that the theme of safeguarding the *depositum fidei* returns in both the first and second letters: "Guard the faith. The faith is to be guarded," he said, emphasizing the words of the apostle: "Beloved Timothy, guard what has been entrusted to you. Avoid the godless chatter, the empty worldly chatter" (cf. 1 Tim 6:20).

The bishop of Rome underscored above all the expression: "guard what has been entrusted to you" and he recalled that "this is our duty. We have all received the gift of faith. We must guard it, at least that it not be watered down, that it continue to be strong with the power of the Holy Spirit who gave it to us."

In this regard, Paul recommended to "rekindle the gift of God" (2 Tim 1:6). After all, Francis said, "if we don't take care, every day, to rekindle this gift of God which is the faith," it "weakens, it becomes watered down, and ends up being a culture: 'Yes, yes, I'm a Christian, yes . . . ,' only a culture. Or a gnosis, an awareness: 'Yes, I know all the matters of the faith well, I know the catechism well." But, the pope asked, "how do you live your faith? This is the importance of rekindling this gift every day: to keep it alive."

Then came a warning against "the spirit of timidity and shame." Indeed, "for God did not give us a spirit of timidity. The spirit of timidity goes against the gift of faith; it doesn't allow it to grow, to go forward, to become great." And shame is the sin of those who say, "Yes, I have faith, but I cover it up, so it isn't plainly seen . . ." It is, the pontiff stated, "like that 'rosewater' faith, as our forebears would say. Because I'm ashamed to live it boldly." But, he emphasized, "this is not faith."

Building on these premises the pope thought that "it would be a good assignment today for all of us to take up this second letter of Paul to Timothy and read it. It's really short, it's easy to read, but it's so beautiful. An elderly bishop's advice to a young bishop; he advises him to lead his church forward: such as guarding the deposit [of faith], such as remembering that faith is a gift that was given to me by the Holy Spirit through my mother, my grandmother, and so many women who have helped."

But why, Francis asked, "is it primarily women who pass on the faith?" The answer is found once again in the testimony of the Blessed Virgin: "Simply because the one who brought us Jesus is a woman. It is the way that Jesus chose. He wanted to have a mother: even the gift of faith passes through women," as it passed "to Jesus through Mary."

The pope thus arrived at his concluding exhortation: "Think about this and if you are able, read this most beautiful second letter to Timothy. And let us ask the Lord for the grace to have sincere faith, a faith which is not negotiated according to the opportunities that are presented. A faith which I try every day to rekindle, or at least which I ask the Holy Spirit to rekindle, and which thus bears great fruit." He then invited us to take home "this advice from Paul to Timothy: 'O Timothy, guard what has been entrusted to you'; in other words, guard this gift."

THE FOOD OF JESUS

Tuesday, January 27, 2015
HEBREWS 10:1–10; MARK 3:31–35

P ray for the desire to follow God's will, to know God's will,
and, once you know it, to go forth with God's will. Pope
Francis recommended this threefold prayer during Mass at St.
Martha's on Tuesday morning.

The pontiff began his reflection from the day's Collect prayer
which asked the Lord: "Guide us to act according to your will, so
that we may bear the fruit of good works." He placed particular
emphasis on the phrase "according to your will," he explained,
because today "this word, 'will,' the will of God, permeates both
of the readings and even the Responsorial Psalm of the liturgy."

It is first seen in the first reading, taken from the letter to the
Hebrews (10:1–10), which "explains the ancient sacrifices and
shows that they are not capable of absolving us. They don't have
the power to give us justice, to forgive sins. They are only a prayer
that the people offer year after year, a request for forgiveness. But
they do not absolve, they have no power."

It returns a second time with "the prophecy" of Psalm 40, in
which St. Paul refers to Christ in order to explain "how the path
of justice began." Indeed, the pope highlighted, "Jesus said, when
he entered the world: 'Sacrifices and offerings thou hast not de-
sired' (Heb 10:5), because they are temporary . . ." Not useless,
but temporary. He continued: "'but a body hast thou prepared for
me; in burnt offerings and sin offerings thou hast taken no pleasure. Then I said, Lo, I have come to do thy will, O God'" (Heb
10:5–7). And "this act of Christ, of coming into the world to do
the will of God, is what absolves us. He is the sacrifice: the true
sacrifice that, once and for all time, has absolved us."

Thus, "Jesus comes to do God's will and begins in a powerful manner, as he ends, on the cross." Indeed, he began his earthly journey by "humbling himself," as Paul writes to the Philippians (2:8): He "emptied himself. He humbled himself, taking the form of a servant, and became obedient unto death on the cross" (cf. 2:7–8). As a result, the pontiff continued, "obedience to God's will is the way of Jesus, who says: 'I come to do the will of God.'" And it is also "the path of holiness, of the Christian, for it was the very path of our absolution: that God, God's plan be realized, that the salvation of God be done." It is the contrary of what happened in the earthly paradise, "with Adam's disobedience." It was that disobedience, Francis specified, which "brought evil to all mankind."

In essence, "sins are also acts of not obeying God, of not doing God's will. However, the Lord teaches us that this is the path, there is no other." A path which "begins with Jesus, in heaven, in the will of obeying the Father" and on "the earth, it begins with Our Lady," at the moment in which she says to the angel: "let it be done to me as you say (cf. Lk 1:38). And with that 'yes' to God, the Lord began his journey among us."

The pope continued to highlight the importance for Jesus of "doing God's will." It is evidenced in the encounter with the Samaritan woman, when "in that southern region, in the heat of that desert zone," when the disciples said to him, "Rabbi, eat," he answered: "No. 'My food is to do the will of the Father'" (cf. Jn 4:31–34). In this manner he made them understand that for him, God's will "was like food, that which gave him strength, that which enabled him to go on." He later explained to the disciples: "I have come into the world to do the will of him who sent me, to fulfill a work of obedience" (cf. Jn 6:38).

Yet, the bishop of Rome observed, even for Jesus it wasn't easy. "The devil, in the temptation in the wilderness, showed him other paths," but they were not the will of the Father and thus "he rejected them." The same thing happens "when Jesus is not understood and they leave him; many disciples leave because they do not understand what God's will is," but Jesus continues to do his will. It is a fidelity which also returns in the words, "Father, thy will be done," which he spoke "before the judgment," when he was praying that evening in the garden, asking God to take away "this cup, this cross. He suffers," the pope said. "Jesus suffers so much. Yet, he says, thy will be done."

This "is the food of Jesus, and it is also the Christian path. He has led us on the path of our life, and doing God's will is not easy, for every day so many options are presented to us on a platter: do this, it's good, it's not bad." We should instead ask ourselves, "Is it God's will? How am I doing in fulfilling God's will?" Thus, the pope offered some practical advice: "First of all ask for grace, pray and ask for the grace of the desire to do God's will. This is a grace."

Next, we must ask ourselves: "Do I pray that the Lord give me the desire to do his will? Or do I look for compromises, because I'm afraid of God's will?" Additionally, he added, we must "pray to know God's will about me and about my life, about the decision that I have to make now, about how to manage things." Thus, in summary, "a prayer to want to do God's will and a prayer to know God's will. And when I know God's will," then there is a third prayer: "to fulfill it. To fulfill that will, which is not mine but his."

Francis knows that all this "isn't easy" and recalled the narrative of the wealthy youth in the gospels of Matthew (19:16–22) and Mark (10:17–22): "that really good boy, whom the gospel says that Jesus loved because he was just. Jesus proposed something else to him but he didn't have the courage." This is why, "when the Father, when Jesus asks something of us," we need to ask ourselves, "Is this his will?" Of course "they are difficult things, and we are not capable, with our strength, of accepting what the Lord tells us." But we can find help by praying: "Lord, give me the courage to go forth according to the Father's will."

The pope concluded by quoting a passage from the gospel of Mark (3:34–35), asking the Lord to "give all of us the grace that one day he may say of us what he said of that group, of that crowd who followed him, those who were seated around him: 'Here are my mother and my brethren! Whoever does the will of God is my brother and sister and mother.' Doing God's will makes us part of Jesus' family. It makes us mother, father, sister, brother." He then asked that "the Lord give us the grace of this familiarity" with him, a familiarity that "means actually doing God's will."

Privatized Salvation

Thursday, January 29, 2015
Hebrews 10:19–25; Mark 4:21–25

God saves us "personally." He saves us "by name" but always included "within a people." During Mass at St. Martha's on Thursday, Pope Francis cautioned against the risk of "privatizing salvation." Indeed "there are forms, there are modes of conduct, that are wrong, and incorrect models of living a Christian life." Referring to the passage from the letter to the Hebrews (10:19–25) read in the morning's liturgy, the pontiff highlighted that if Jesus truly "inaugurated a new way of life" and "we must follow it," then it is also true that "we must follow it how the Lord wants, according to the form that he wants," and not by the incorrect model of those who tend to "privatize salvation."

Indeed, the pope explained, Jesus "saved all of us, but not generically. Everyone, each one, by first and last name." And this is "personal salvation." Each of us can say it is "for me," because "the Lord looked at me, gave his life for me, opened this door, this new way for me." There is, however, the "risk of forgetting that he saved us" not only "individually, but within a people," for "the Lord always saves us within a people." When the Lord "calls Abraham, he promises to create a people." And this is why we read in the letter to the Hebrews: "Let us consider . . . one another." If, Francis emphasized, I interpret salvation as being "salvation for me alone," then "I'm going the wrong way: privatizing salvation is the wrong way."

But "what are the criteria in order not to privatize salvation?" They can be found precisely in the passage from the reading. There is, "first of all, the criterion of faith," the pope explained. "Faith in Jesus purifies us"; and then "let us draw near with a true heart in full assurance of faith, with our hearts sprinkled clean from an evil conscience." The first criterion, therefore, is "the sign of faith, the path of faith." There is then another criterion which lies in "an oft-forgotten virtue: 'hope.'" Indeed, we must maintain "the confession of our hope without wavering," which is "like the handmaid: it is what leads us forward, enables us to see the promises and go forward." Finally, the third criterion is "love": we must make sure that we "consider one another, stir up one another to love and good works."

A concrete example, the pontiff said, can be found in parish or community life: when "I'm there, I can privatize salvation" if I am there "only socially." To avoid this risk, "I must ask myself: when I speak, do I communicate faith; [when] I speak, do I communicate hope; [when] I speak, do I practice and communicate love?" Because "if, in a community, we don't speak, we don't encourage one another in these three virtues, the members of that community have privatized the faith."

Here is the error: "Each one seeks his own salvation, not the salvation of all, the salvation of the people." Yet "Jesus saved each one, but within a people, within a church." At that point it happens that "you are saved, but not as the Lord saved you." In this regard, the author of the letter to Hebrews "provides important advice: let us not stay away from our assembly." It is practical advice, which the pope paused to explain: it happens, in fact, "when we assemble—in the parish, in a group—and we judge others," by saying: "I don't like this . . . I come because I have to come, but I don't like it . . ."; we end up "staying away." What emerges is "a sort of scorn toward others." And this is not the door, the new and living way that the Lord has opened, has inaugurated.

This also happened in the first years of the church. Paul, for example, "rebukes those who go to meetings to serve the Eucharist and also have lunch, but among themselves, leaving the others there. They scorn the others; they stay away from the entire community; they stay away from the people of God." In reality, "they privatized salvation," thinking, "salvation is for me and for my small group, but not for the whole of the people of God."

This, the pontiff recalled, "is a really big mistake. It's what we call and see as the ecclesial elite." It happens when "among the people of God, small groups are created" who "think they are good Christians" and might even have "good will, but they are groups that have privatized salvation."

For this reason, Francis recapitulated, "if I am in my parish, in my group, in my family," the criteria for recognizing "whether I am a true child of the church, a child of God, saved by Jesus, within his people, are: if I speak of faith, if I speak of hope, if I speak of love." But be careful: "when in a group we talk about many things and we don't mutually give one another strength, we don't do good works," then we "end up neglecting the large group in order to form small groups of the elite." However, God "saves us within a people, not among the elite, which we have created with our philosophy or our way of understanding the faith."

Thus, we must ask ourselves, "Do I tend to privatize salvation for myself, for my group, for my elite?" Or ask, "Do I not neglect the people of God as a whole, do I not fall away from the people of God, even if I am always in the community, in the family, with the language of faith, of hope, and the language of works of love?" The pope concluded by asking "that the Lord give us the grace to always feel we are the people of God, saved personally." For the truth is that "he saves us by name," but "within a people, not within the small group I create for myself."

First Love

Friday, January 30, 2015
Hebrews 10:32–39; Mark 4:26–34

"Never forget that first love," which is "the joy of the first encounter with Jesus." This means we need to constantly nourish our hope. And these "two parameters," memory and hope, are the only "framework" in which a Christian can experience "salvation, which is always a gift of God," without falling into the temptation of being "lukewarm," like those who, along with their memory, have also lost hope and enthusiasm. Thus, Francis advised that we not remain "halfway," as he celebrated Mass at St. Martha's on Friday morning.

"The salvation of the righteous is from the Lord" (Ps 37[36]:39). This psalm verse, the pope pointed out, reminds us of the truth that "salvation is a gift the Lord gives": it can't be bought or obtained through study, for it is always "a gift, a present." But the real question is, "How to protect this salvation? What to do so this salvation remains in us and bears fruit, as Jesus explains, like a seed or kernel of mustard?" With this, Francis referred to the day's reading from the gospel according to Mark (4:26–35).

And from the passage from the letter to the Hebrews (10:32–39), read during the Mass, the pope underscored that "there are criteria to protect this present, this gift of salvation, in order to allow this salvation to go forth and bear its fruit in us."

The "first criterion," the pope explained, "is that of memory." In fact, we read in the text: "Brethren, recall the former days, after you received the light of Christ." Those are "the days of the first love," as the prophets say: it is "the day of the encounter with Jesus." Because, Francis remarked, "when we encountered Jesus," or better yet, he indicated, when "he let himself be encountered by us, for it is he who does all"—"it brought great joy, the will to do great things," as the same author of the letter explains. Therefore, the first criterion to protect the gift of salvation is "not to forget those first days" marked by "certain enthusiasm." Most of all, "do not forget" that "first love."

The writer of the letter to the Hebrews then goes on, emphasizing the "joy that enabled you to bear all things," to a point when "all seemed meagre in those former days, and one went forth with enthusiasm." He continued: the letter "exhorts us not to abandon that courage—namely 'this honesty'—that parrhesìa of those former days." It is indeed that "first love" that "made grow within us that courage, that 'let's go on!,' that enthusiasm."

The call, however, is to "not abandon honesty." But, "abandon" is not even the "right word," Francis noted, indicating that if "we go to the original text" we find a powerful expression: "Do not throw away, do not waste, do not reject honesty." It is "like a rejection: do not push away this honesty, this courage, the courage of the former days."

"This is why memory is so important, to remember the grace received," the pope stated. Indeed, "if we push away this enthusiasm that comes from our memory of that first love, this enthusiasm that comes from the first love," then what comes is "that serious danger to Christians: warmth." For "lukewarm Christians stay there, idle; and yes, they are Christians, but they have forgotten that first love, they have lost their enthusiasm." What's more, "lukewarm Christians have also lost patience, that 'tolerating' things in life with the spirit of Jesus' love; that 'tolerating,' that bearing difficulties 'on one's shoulders.'" This is why, the bishop of Rome stated, "lukewarm Christians, the poor souls, are in grave danger."

In this regard, Francis suggested, "there are two images which really strike me," and of which each person should be warned: "But you are lukewarm, be careful!" St. Peter, in his second letter, uses "the image of the dog who turns back to its own vomit." And "this image is distasteful," the pope acknowledged. However, it is a fitting example of "the lukewarm Christian" who returns to that "first love, as if that love never existed."

"The second image, also unpleasant," he warned, "is the one that Jesus recounts of the person who wants to follow him, and does follow him, and then he casts out the demon." This demon, who has gone out of the man, "passes through the desert" with the intention of returning "to that man, to that woman" from which he came. And when he "returns, he finds the house in order, clean and nice." Thus "he gets angry, goes, looks for seven demons worse than him and returns" to take "possession of that house." And in this way "the person isn't wounded," because it involves "'polite' demons, who even knock on the door to come in, but they do come in." The same happens to "a lukewarm Christian" who "doesn't know who is knocking at the door and opens it," even saying "come in!" But, Jesus says, in the end, "that soul ends up even worse than before."

"These two images of the warmth of the Christian make us think," the pontiff said. This way we must never "forget our first love"; rather, we should always "remember that first love." This is why the answer to the question "how do I go on?" is: "with hope." That is what the letter to the Hebrews says to every Christian: "For yet a little while, and the coming one shall come and shall not tarry."

And thus there are "two parameters" available to the Christian: "memory and hope." Ultimately it means "reclaiming the memory so as not to lose that most beautiful experience of the first love that nourishes our hope." So often, the pope admitted, "hope is dark." But the Christian "goes forward. He believes. He goes, for he knows that hope does not disappoint, to find Jesus."

"These two parameters," he continued, "are the very framework in which we are able to protect this salvation of the righteous which comes from the Lord, this gift of the Lord." We must protect this salvation, "for the little mustard seed to grow and bear its fruit." However, Francis continued, many Christians, "cause pain, create heartache—so many Christians!" They are the many Christians who go "halfway" and "fail along this path toward the encounter with Jesus." Even if the journey "began with the encounter with Jesus," in the middle of the road, "they have lost the memory of that first love and have no hope."

The pope asked the Lord for "the grace to protect the present, the gift of salvation." It is a gift that each Christian must protect "on this journey that always reclaims the memory and hope." But, he concluded, "he alone can give us this grace. May he send us the Holy Spirit to walk on this path."

The Gospel in Hand

Tuesday, February 3, 2015
Hebrews 12:1–4; Mark 5:21–43

Read a page of the gospel every day, for "ten, fifteen minutes and no more." Keep your "eyes fixed on Jesus" in order to imagine yourself "in the scene and to speak with Jesus" about what comes from the heart. These are the characteristics of "contemplative prayer," a true source of hope for our life. Pope Francis offered this recommendation during Mass at St. Martha's on Tuesday morning.

In the first reading (Heb 12:1–4), Francis noted, the author of the letter to the Hebrews refers to the memory of the first days after conversion, after the encounter with Jesus, and also refers to the memory of our fathers: "how much they suffered when they were on the journey." The author, "looking to these fathers, says: we too 'are surrounded by so great a cloud of witnesses.'" Thus, it is "the testimony of our ancestors" that he recalls. And "he also recalls our experience, when we were so happy in the first encounter with Jesus." This "is the memory that we spoke about as a point of reference for Christian life."

But today, the pope remarked, "the author of the letter speaks about another point of reference, namely, hope." And "he tells us that we must have the courage to go forward: 'let us persevere in running the race that lies before us.'" Then "he says what is the very core of hope: 'keeping our eyes fixed on Jesus.'" This is the point: "if we don't keep our eyes fixed on Jesus it is difficult for us to have hope." We can perhaps be "optimistic, be positive, but hope?"

After all, Francis explained, "hope is learned only by looking to Jesus, contemplating Jesus; we learn through contemplative prayer." This was what he wished "to talk about today," fueling his reflection with a question: "I can ask you: how do you pray?" Someone, he said, might respond, "Father, I say the prayers I learned as a child." And he said, "Okay, this is good." Someone else might add: "I pray the rosary too, every day!" And the pope confirmed: "It's good to pray the rosary every day." And finally, one might say, "I also talk with the Lord, when I have a problem, or with Our Lady or with the saints . . ." And "this is good" too.

With regard to all of this, the pontiff posed another question: "Do you pray in contemplation?" The question might throw us a curve, and someone might ask, "What is this, Father? What is this prayer? Where can we buy it? How do we do it?" Francis' answer is simple: "It can be done only with the gospel in hand." Basically, he said, "you pick up the gospel, select a passage, read it once, read it twice; imagine, as if you see what is happening, and contemplate Jesus."

To provide some practical guidance, the pope gave an example from the day's liturgy, a passage from the gospel according to Mark (5:21–43), which "teaches us many beautiful things." Beginning from this page, he asked, "How do I contemplate with today's gospel?" And, sharing his personal experience, he proposed the first reflection: "I see that Jesus was in the midst of the crowd; there was a great crowd around him. The word 'crowd' is used five times in this passage. But doesn't Jesus rest? I can imagine: always with the crowd! Most of Jesus' life is spent on the street, with the crowd. Doesn't he rest? Yes, once: the gospel says that he slept on the boat, but the storm came and the disciples woke him. Jesus was constantly among the people."

For this reason, the pope suggested, "we look to Jesus this way, I contemplate Jesus this way, I imagine Jesus this way. And I say to Jesus whatever comes to my mind to say to him."

Francis continued his meditation with these words: "Then, in the midst of the crowd, there was that sick woman, and Jesus was aware. But how did Jesus, in the middle of so many people, realize that a woman had touched him?" And, indeed, he asked directly, "Who touched me?" The disciples, in return, pointed out to Jesus: "You see the crowd pressing around you, and yet you say, 'Who touched me?'" The question, Francis emphasized, is that "Jesus not only understands the crowd, feels the crowd, but he hears the beating of each one of our hearts, of each one of us. He cares for all and for each one, always!"

The pope, continuing to reread the passage from Mark, explained that the same situation happens again when the ruler of the synagogue approaches Jesus "to tell him about his gravely ill little daughter. And he leaves everything to tend to this one: Jesus in the great and in the small, always!" Then, Francis continued, "we can go on and see that he arrives at the house. He sees that tumult, those women who were called to mourn over the dead body, wailing, weeping." But Jesus says, "Don't worry: she's sleeping!" And in response to these words, some even begin to scoff at him. However, "he stays quiet," and with his patience he manages to bear this situation, to avoid responding to those who mock him.

The gospel account culminates with "the little girl's resurrection." And Jesus, "rather than saying 'Praised be God!' says to them: 'Please, give her something to eat.'" For Jesus "always has the fine details in front of him," the pope explained.

"What I did with this gospel," Francis explained, "is contemplative prayer: to pick up the gospel, read, and imagine myself in the scene, to imagine what's happening and speak with Jesus" about what "comes from my heart." And with this, he continued, "we allow hope to grow, because we have our eyes fixed on Jesus." Then he proposed: "Pray in contemplation." And even if we have many commitments, he said, we can always find the time, even fifteen minutes at home. "Pick up the gospel, a short passage, imagine what is happening and talk to Jesus about it." This way "your eyes will be fixed on Jesus, and not so much on soap operas, for example. Your ears will be fixed on the words of Jesus and not so much on the neighbors' gossip."

"Contemplative prayer helps us to hope" and teaches us "to live from the substance of the gospel, the bishop of Rome persisted. And this is why we must "always pray: say prayers, pray the rosary, speak with the Lord, but also carry out this contemplative prayer in order to keep our eyes fixed on Jesus." From here "comes hope." And also this way, "our Christian life moves within that framework, between memory and hope: the memory of the entire past journey, the memory of so many graces received from the Lord; and hope, looking to the Lord, who is the only One who can give me hope." And "to look to the Lord, to know the Lord, we pick up the gospel and we pray in contemplation."

In closing, Francis again repeated the experience of praying in contemplation: "Today, for example," he suggested, "find ten minutes, fifteen minutes and no more. Read the gospel, imagine and speak with Jesus. And nothing more. And in this way, your knowledge of Jesus will be greater and your hope will grow. Don't forget, keeping your eyes fixed on Jesus." This is why we call it "contemplative prayer."

I WILL CURE YOU

Thursday, February 5, 2015
MARK 6:7–13

The church's true mission is not to develop an efficient aid mechanism, modeled after an NGO (nongovernmental organization). The profile of an apostle—who in simplicity and poverty proclaims the gospel with the one true power that comes from God—is recognized instead in the plain words that Jesus recommends to the disciples returning with joy from their mission: "we are unworthy servants." And thus, at Mass at St. Martha's on Thursday the pope reaffirmed that the true mission of the church is "healing the wounds of the heart, opening doors, forgiving all, liberating, and saying that God is good, forgives all, is Father; God is gentle and always waits for us."

In the passage from the gospel according to Mark (6:7–13) offered in today's liturgy, the pontiff began, "We heard that Jesus called his disciples" and sent them "to take the gospel; it is he who calls." The gospel recounts that he called them to him, sent them, and gave them power. "In the vocation of the disciples, the Lord gives power: the power to cast out impure spirits, to liberate, to heal. This is the power that Jesus gives." Indeed, he "does not give the power to maneuver or to build large companies"; but "the power, the same power that he had, the power that he received from the Father, he conveys to them." And he does so with "plain advice: go into the community, but do not take anything for the journey except a staff; no bread, no bag, no money . . . in poverty!"

The gospel, Francis stated, "is so very rich and so powerful that it does not need to create large firms, big companies, in order to be proclaimed." For the gospel "should be proclaimed in poverty, and a real pastor is one who goes like Jesus: poor, to proclaim the gospel, with that power." And "when the gospel is safeguarded with this simplicity, with this poverty, one clearly sees that salvation is not a theology of prosperity" but rather "a gift, the same gift that Jesus had received in order to give."

Francis again proposed "that most beautiful scene in the synagogue, when Jesus introduces himself: 'I was sent to bring salvation, to bring glad tidings to the poor, liberation to the incarcerated, to the blind the gift of sight. Liberation to all those who are oppressed and to proclaim the year of grace, the year of joy.' This," the pope said, is precisely "the aim of the gospel message, without many curious, worldly things." This is how Jesus conveys it.

And what, the pope asked, does Jesus "command" the disciples to do, "what is his pastoral plan?" It is simply to "cure, heal, raise, liberate, cast out demons: this is the simple plan." It coincides, Francis pointed out, with "the mission of the church: the church which heals, which cures." Such that, he recalled, "a few times I have spoken of the church as a field hospital; it's true! How many wounded there are, how many wounded! How many people who need their wounds to be healed!"

Thus, the pope continued, "this is the church's mission: healing the wounds of the heart, opening doors, liberating, and saying that God is good, that God forgives all, that God is Father, that God is gentle, that God always waits for us."

Referring to the gospel of Luke (10:17–20), the pontiff remarked that "the disciples returned with joy" from their mission, because "they didn't believe they would have succeeded." And "they said to the Lord: 'Lord, even the demons left!'" They were "joyful because this power of Jesus, employed with simplicity, with poverty, with love, produced a good result."

The very phrase that Jesus addressed to the joyful disciples, according to the gospel, "explains everything." They recounted: "We did this, and this, and this, and this . . ." Thus, after listening to them, Jesus closes his eyes and says: "I saw Satan fall like lightning from heaven." The words reveal "the struggle of the church: it's true, we should get help and create aid organizations, for the Lord gives us gifts for this"; but, the pope warned, "when we forget this mission, forget about poverty, forget apostolic zeal and put our hope in these means, the church slowly lapses into an NGO and becomes a fine organization: powerful but not evangelical, because that spirit is lacking, that poverty, that healing power."

There is more: on their return, Jesus brings the disciples with him "to rest a little, to have a day in the country, to have sandwiches and soft drinks." The Lord wants "to spend a little time together to celebrate." And together they talk about the mission they have just done. But Jesus doesn't tell them: "'You're great, eh! Now let's plan things better for the next excursion!'" He limits himself to recommending: "'When you have done all that is commanded you, say, We are unworthy servants'" (Lk 17:10).

In these words, Francis remarked, the Lord described the profile of an apostle. Indeed, "what would be the greatest praise for an apostle?" The answer: "He was a laborer for the kingdom, he was a worker for the kingdom." Indeed, "this is the highest praise, because he goes on Jesus' path of proclamation; he goes to heal, to safeguard, to proclaim these glad tidings and this year of grace. To enable the people to find the Father once again, to make peace in the people's hearts."

The pope concluded with an invitation to read this gospel passage, emphasizing "the most important things to Jesus, in proclaiming the gospel: they are these, these small virtues." And "then it is he, it is the Holy Spirit who does it all."

THE GREAT ONE'S DARKEST HOUR

Friday, February 6, 2015
MARK 6:14–29

On Friday during Mass at St. Martha's, Pope Francis spoke about John the Baptist: the man and the way. The way that John indicated was that of Jesus, to which we too are all called at the moment of truth.

The pope began his reflection speaking about "the great John" who, according to Jesus, was "the greatest man born of woman." The day's passage from Mark's gospel (6:14–29) speaks about the imprisonment and martyrdom of John, who was a "man faithful to his mission; a man who suffered many temptations" and "never, ever betrayed his vocation." He was a faithful man "of great authority, respected by everyone: the great one of that time."

Then Pope Francis paused to analyze the character of John the Baptist. "What came out of his mouth was just. His heart was just." He was so great that "Jesus would say that 'Elijah returned to clean house, to prepare the way.'" And John "was aware that his duty was simply to proclaim, to proclaim the coming of the Messiah. He was aware," Francis added, reflecting on what St. Augustine said, "that he was only the voice, the Word was another." And when "he was tempted to 'steal' this truth, he remained just: 'It is not me; he is coming after me. I am the servant; I am the manservant; I am the one who opens the doors, in order that he may come.'"

The pontiff thus introduced the concept of "the way," because, he recalled, "John is the forerunner, the forerunner not only of the Lord's entry into public life, but of the entire life of the Lord." The Baptist "goes forth on the Lord's path, bears witness of the Lord not only by indicating—'He is the one!'—but also leading life to the end as the Lord did." Through his martyrdom, he became the "forerunner of the life and death of Jesus Christ."

The pope continued to reflect on these parallel paths along which "the great one" suffers "so many trials and becomes small, so very small until scorned." John, like Jesus, "abases himself; he knows the way of abasement. John with all that authority, thinking of his life, comparing it with that of Jesus, tells the people who [Jesus] is, how his life will be: 'It is fitting that he grow; however I must become small.'" And this, the pope underscored, is "John's life: to become small before Christ, so that Christ may grow." It is "the life of the servant who makes room, makes way for the Lord to come."

John's life "was not easy." Indeed, "when Jesus began his public life," he was "close to the Essenes, that is, to the observers of the law, but also of prayers, of penance." Thus, at a certain point, during the period that John was incarcerated, "he suffered the trial of darkness, of his soul's darkest hour." And that scene, Francis commented, "is moving: the great one, the greatest one sent two disciples to Jesus, to ask him: 'John asks you, Are you he who is to come or shall we look for another?'" Thus, along John's path appeared "the darkness of mistake, the darkness of life burnt out in error. And for him, this was a cross."

To John's question "Jesus responds with the words of Isaiah." The Baptist "understands, but his heart remains in darkness." Nevertheless, John agrees to the requests of the king "who enjoys listening to him, and who enjoys an adulterous life." John "almost becomes a preacher of the court, of this confused king." But "he humiliated himself" because he "thought to convert this man."

In the end, the pope said, "after this purification, after this continuous descent into annihilation, leading to the annihilation of Jesus, his life ends." That confused king "is able to make a decision, but not because his heart is converted," but rather "because wine gives him courage."

And thus John's life is ended "under the authority of a mediocre, drunken, and corrupt king, because of a dancer's whim and because of the vindictive hatred of an adulterous woman." Thus "the great one meets his end, the greatest man born of woman," Francis stated. He then shared: "When I read this passage, I am moved." And he added a thought, useful for the spiritual life of every Christian: "I think about two things: first, I think about our martyrs, today's martyrs, those men, women, children who are persecuted, hated, driven from their homes, tortured, massacred." And this, he underlined, "is not a thing of the past: this is happening today. Our martyrs meet their end under the authority of corrupt people who hate Jesus Christ." For this reason, "it will do us good to think about our martyrs. Today we think of Paul Miki, but that happened in 1600. Let us think of those of today, of 2015."

The pontiff continued, indicating that this passage also urges us to reflect on our own life: "I too will meet my end. We all will. No one can 'buy' life. We too, willingly or unwillingly, are traveling the road of life's existential annihilation." And this, he said, impels us "to pray that this annihilation may resemble as much as possible that of Jesus Christ, his annihilation."

Francis' meditation thus came full circle: "John, the great one, who diminishes endlessly into nothingness; the martyrs, who are diminishing today, in our church today, into nothingness; and we, who are on this road and heading toward the ground, where we will all end up." And thus the pope's final prayer: "May the Lord illuminate us, enable us to understand this way of John, the forerunner of Jesus; the way of Jesus who teaches us how ours has to be."

Working with God

Monday, February 9, 2015
Genesis 1:1–19; Mark 6:53–56

God is always working through love, and it is up to us to respond to him with responsibility and in the spirit of reconciliation, which gives way to the Holy Spirit. Pope Francis addressed this invitation during Mass on Monday morning in the chapel of St. Martha's.

The Holy Father began his reflection by referring to a passage from Genesis (1:1–19). "Today's Liturgy of the Word leads us to think, to meditate on the works of God: God works." In fact, "Jesus himself said: 'My Father still works, still acts, still operates; so do I!'" And in this way, the pope pointed out that "some medieval theologians explained: first God, the Creator, creates the universe, creates the heavens, the earth, the living beings. He creates. The work of creation." However, "creation is not the end: he continuously supports what he created, works to sustain what he created in order that it continue."

In the gospel of Mark (6:53–56), the pope indicated, "we see 'the other creation' of God," namely, "that of Jesus who comes to 're-create' what has been ruined by sin." And "we see Jesus among the people." Indeed, Mark writes, "'when they got out of the boat, immediately the people recognized him, and ran about the whole neighborhood and began to bring sick people on their pallets to any place where they heard he was.' And those who touched him were saved." This is the "re-creation," and "the liturgy expresses the soul of the church in this, when the beautiful prayer is said: 'O God, that you created the universe so wondrously, but more wondrously you created redemption.'" Thus, "this 'second creation' is more wondrous than the first, this second work is more wondrous."

There is then, Francis continued, "another work: the work of persevering in the faith, which Jesus says is done by the Holy Spirit: 'I will send the Paraclete and he will teach you and remind you; he will make you remember what I have said.'" It is "the work of the Spirit within us, to keep the word of Jesus alive, to preserve creation, to guarantee that this creation does not die." Thus "the presence there of the Spirit, who keeps the first creation and the second alive."

In other words, "God works. He continues to work and we can ask ourselves how we should respond to this creation of God, which was born from love because he works through love." Thus, "to the 'first creation' we must respond with the responsibility the Lord gives us: 'The earth is yours, foster it; make it grow!'" For this reason, "we too have the responsibility to make the earth flourish, to make creation flourish, to safeguard it and make it flourish according to its laws. We are lords of creation, not masters." And we mustn't "take control of creation, but foster it, faithful to its laws." Indeed, "this is the first response to God's work: work to safeguard creation, to make it fruitful."

From this perspective, the pope continued, "when we hear people hold meetings to consider how to safeguard creation, we could say: 'No, they are green!'" Instead, he suggested, "they aren't green: this is Christian!" And this "is our response to God's 'first creation,' it is our responsibility!" In fact, "a Christian who doesn't safeguard creation, who doesn't make it flourish, is a Christian who isn't concerned with God's work, that work born of God's love for us." And "this is the first response to the first creation: safeguard creation, make it flourish."

But, Pope Francis asked, "how do we respond to the 'second creation'?" In this regard, he said that "Paul the apostle tells us the right word, which is the true response: 'Let yourselves reconcile with God.'" This, he explained, is "that open interior attitude for going constantly on the path of inner reconciliation, of community reconciliation, because reconciliation is Christ's work." And Paul also says: "God has reconciled the world in Christ." Thus, "to the 'second creation' we say: 'Yes, we must let ourselves reconcile with the Lord.'"

Francis then posed another question: "And to the work that the Holy Spirit does within us, of reminding us of Jesus' word, of explaining to us, of making us understand what Jesus said: how do we respond?" It is again "Paul who tells us" not to grieve "the Holy Spirit who is within you: be attentive, he is your guest; he is within you; he works within you! Do not grieve the Holy Spirit." And this is "in order that we believe in a personal God. God is person; he is the person of Father, the person of Son, the person of the Holy Spirit." After all, "all three are engaged in this recreation, in this re-creation, in this perseverance in re-creation." Therefore, our response to all three is "to safeguard creation and make it flourish, to let ourselves reconcile with Jesus, with God in Jesus, in Christ, each day; and do not grieve the Holy Spirit, do not push him away: he is the guest in our heart, the One who accompanies us, who makes us grow."

In conclusion, the pope prayed that "the Lord give us the grace to understand that he is at work; and give us the grace to respond rightly to this work of love."

Two Identity Cards

Tuesday, February 10, 2015
Genesis 1:20–2:4; Mark 7:1–13

To know our true identity we cannot be "seated Christians" but must have the "courage to always take up the journey to seek the Lord's face," because we are the "image of God." In the Mass celebrated at St. Martha's on Tuesday morning expounding on the day's first reading—the creation narrative from the book of Genesis (1:20–2:4)—Pope Francis reflected on a question essential for every person: "Who am I?"

Our "identity card," the pope said, is found in the fact that mankind was created "in the image, in the likeness of God." But then, he added, "the question we could ask ourselves is, How can I know the image of God? How can I know what he is like in order to know what I'm like? Where can I find the image of God?" The answer obviously cannot be found "on a computer, nor in an encyclopedia, nor in books," because "God's image is not in any catalogue." There is only one way "to find the image of God, which is my identity" and that is to journey: "If we don't take up the journey, we will never get to know the face of God."

This desire for knowledge is also found in the Old Testament. The psalmists, Francis pointed out, "say many times: I want to see your face"; and "even Moses says this once to the Lord." But in reality "it isn't easy, because taking up the journey means letting go of many securities, many opinions about what God's image is like, and to seek it." It means, in other words, "to let God and life put us to the test." It means taking a risk, for "only in this way can we manage to know the face of God, the image of God: to take up the journey."

The pope drew again on the Old Testament to recall that "the people of God did this, the prophets did this." For instance, "the great Elijah: after he wins and purifies the faith of Israel, he hears the queen's threat and is afraid and doesn't know what to do. He takes up the journey. And at a certain point, he would rather die." But God "calls him, gives him food and drink, and says: keep going." This is how Elijah "comes to the mount and there he finds God." His was thus "a long journey, an arduous journey, a difficult journey," but it teaches us that "those who don't take up the journey will never know the image of God, will never find the face of God." It's a lesson for all of us: "seated Christians, calm Christians," the pope stated, "will not know the face of God." They have the presumption to say, "God is like this, and like this . . ." But in reality "they do not know him."

To journey, instead, we need to have "that restlessness, which God placed in our heart and which carries us onward to seek him." The same thing happened, the pontiff explained, "to Job who, with his trials, began to think, What kind of God would let this happen to me?" His friends too, "after days of great silence, began to talk, to argue with him." But none of this was helpful. "With these arguments, Job did not know God." Instead, "when he allowed himself to be questioned by the Lord in the trial, he meets God." And from Job we are also able to hear "that word that will help us so much on this journey to find our identity: 'I had heard of thee by the hearing of the ear, but now my eye sees thee.'" And this, according to Pope Francis, is the heart of the matter: "the encounter with God" that can happen "only by taking up the journey."

Of course, he continued, "Job took up the journey cursing." He actually "had the courage to curse life and his history: 'Let the day perish wherein I was born . . .'" In essence, the pope reflected, "sometimes, on the journey of life, we don't find the meaning of things." The prophet Jeremiah had the same experience. "After being seduced by the Lord, he felt that curse: 'Why me?'" He wanted to "remain calmly seated" but instead "the Lord wanted to show him his face."

This applies to each of us: "to know our identity, to know the image of God, we must take up the journey"; we must be "restless, not calm." This is precisely what it means "to seek the face of God."

Pope Francis then referred to the passage from Mark's gospel (7:1–13) in which "Jesus meets people who are afraid to take up the journey" and who create a sort of "caricature of God." But that "is a false identity card" because, the pontiff explained, "these non-restless ones have calmed the restlessness of their heart, by illustrating God with commandments." But in doing so "they have forgotten God" and see only "the tradition of men." And, "when they have uncertainty, they invent or make up another commandment." Jesus says to the scribes and Pharisees who accumulate commandments: "you are 'thus making void the word of God through your tradition which you hand on. And many such things you do.'" This "is the false identity card, which we might have without taking up the journey," remaining "calm, without restlessness of heart."

In this regard the pope highlighted a particular "curiosity": in fact, the Lord "praises them but reprimands them where it hurts the most. He praises them: 'You have a fine way of rejecting the commandment of God, in order to keep your tradition.'" But then "he reprimands them there, at the most powerful point of the commandments with one's neighbor." In fact, Jesus recalls that Moses said, "Honor your father and your mother; and he who speaks evil of father or mother, let him surely die." He continues: "but you say instead that if a man tells his father or his mother, that what I would give to help you, namely, to feed you, to clothe you, to buy you medicine, 'is Corban' (that is, given to God)—then you no longer permit him to do anything for his father or mother." In doing so "they wash their hands according to the mildest commandment, [yet] the strongest one, the only one with a promise of blessing." And so, "they are at peace, they are calm, they do not take up the journey." This, then, "is the image of God that they have." In reality their journey is "in quotation marks," in other words, "a journey that doesn't move, a still journey. They deny their parents but fulfill the laws of the tradition they have made."

Concluding his reflection, the bishop of Rome again compared the two readings to "two identity cards." The first is "the one we all have, because the Lord made us like this"; it is "the one that tells us: take up the journey and you will know your identity, for you are the image of God; you were created in the likeness of God. Take up the journey and look for God." The other, however, reassures us: "No, relax: fulfill all these commandments and this is God. This is the face of God." The pope then asked the Lord to "give everyone the grace of courage to always take up the journey, to seek the Lord's face, that face which we will see one day, but which we must look for here on Earth."

As Martyrs

Tuesday, February 17, 2015

The Holy Father offered Mass at St. Martha's for the 21 Copts killed in Libya

Genesis 6:5–8; 7:1–5, 10; Mark 8:14–21

"We offer this Mass for our twenty-one Coptic brothers, slaughtered for the sole reason that they were Christians." These were Pope Francis' words during the Mass celebrated at St. Martha's on Tuesday, February 17. "Let us pray for them, that the Lord welcome them as martyrs, for their families, for my brother Tawadros, who is suffering greatly," he added.

In a telephone conversation on Monday afternoon, Pope Francis spoke personally with Tawadros II, Patriarch of the Coptic Orthodox Church. He expressed his profound sadness for the barbaric assassination carried out by Islamic fundamentalists and assured him of his prayers for the funerals.

Pope Francis opened his homily with the words of the entrance antiphon, "Be my protector, O God, a mighty stronghold to save me. For you are my rock, my stronghold! Lead me, guide me, for the sake of your name" (cf. Ps 31[30]:3–4). He continued with the passage on the flood in the day's reading from the book of Genesis (6:5–8; 7:1–5, 10) which, he said, "makes us think about man's capacity for destruction: man is capable of destroying everything that God made" when "he thinks he is more powerful than God." Thus, "God can make good things, but man is capable of destroying them all."

Even starting from the beginning "in the first chapters of the Bible, we find many examples." For example, Francis explained, "man summons the flood through his wickedness; it is he who summons it!" Moreover, "man summons the fire out of heaven, to Sodom and Gomorrah, out of his wickedness." Then, "man creates confusion, the division of humanity—Babel, the Tower of Babel—with his wickedness." In other words, "man is capable of destruction; we are all capable of destruction." This is confirmed again in Genesis with "a very, very sharp phrase: 'This wickedness was great and every innermost intent of their heart—in the heart of mankind—was nothing but evil, always.'"

It isn't a question of being too negative, the pope pointed out, because "this is the truth." At this point, "we are even capable of destroying fraternity," as demonstrated by the story of "Cain and Abel in the first pages of the Bible." This episode, which "destroys fraternity, is the beginning of wars: jealousy, envy, such greed for power, to have more power." Yes, Francis confirmed, "this seems negative, but it is realistic." After all, he added, one need only pick up a newspaper to see "that more than ninety percent of the news is about destruction—more than ninety percent! And we see this every day!"

Thus, the fundamental question: "What happens in the heart of man?" the pope asked. "Jesus once warned his disciples that evil does not enter a man's heart because he eats something that isn't pure, but rather it comes out of the heart." And "all wickedness comes out of the heart of man." Indeed, "our weak heart is wounded." There is "always that desire for autonomy" that leads one to say: "I do what I want, and if I want to do this, I do it! And if I want to make war over this, I do it! And if I want to destroy my family over this, I do it! And if I want to kill my neighbor over this, I do it!" But this is really "everyday news," the pope remarked, observing that "newspapers don't tell us news about the life of saints."

Therefore, he continued, returning to the central question, "Why are we like this?" And the answer: "because we have the opportunity to destroy. This is the problem!" And in doing so, "with war, with arms trafficking, we are entrepreneurs of death!" And "there are countries that sell arms to this one that is at war with that one, and they also sell them to that one, so that war continues." The problem is precisely the "capacity for destruction and this does not come from our neighbor" but "from us!"

"Every innermost intent of the heart is nothing but evil," Francis again repeated. And "we have this seed inside, this possibility." But "we also have the Holy Spirit who saves us." It is thus a matter of choosing to start with the "little things." And so, "when a woman goes to the market and finds another, starts to gossip, to speak ill of her neighbor, about that woman over there: this woman kills, this woman is evil." And this happens "at the market" but also "in the parish, in associations, when there is jealousy; the envious ones go to the priest to say 'this one no, this one yes, this one does . . .'" And this too "is evil, the capacity to destroy, which all of us have."

This is the point on which "today the church, on the threshold of Lent, causes us to reflect." The pope's reflection in this regard started from the gospel of Mark (8:14–21). "In the gospel, Jesus lightly reprimands the disciples who were arguing: 'you were supposed to bring the bread—no, you were!'" Basically, the Twelve "were discussing as usual, were arguing amongst themselves." And Jesus says something beautiful to them: "Take heed, beware of the leaven of the Pharisees and the leaven of Herod." Thus, "he simply makes an example of two people: Herod is bad, he is an assassin, and the Pharisees hypocrites." But the Lord also speaks of "'leaven' and they do not understand."

The fact is, as Mark writes, the disciples "were speaking about bread, about this bread, and Jesus tells them, 'That leaven is dangerous; what we have inside is what leads us to destroy. Take heed, beware!'" Then "Jesus shows the other door: 'Are your hearts hardened? Do you not remember when I broke the five loaves, the door of God's salvation?'" In fact, "nothing good ever comes from arguing," he said. "There will always be division, destruction!" He continued: "Think about salvation, about what God too did for us, and make the right choice!" But the disciples "did not understand because their hearts were hardened by this passion, by this wickedness of arguing amongst themselves to see who was to blame for forgetting the bread."

Francis then advised that "this message of the Lord" should be taken seriously, because "this isn't something strange, this isn't a Martian talking, no: these are things that happen in everyday life." And to confirm this, he repeated, we only need to pick up "the newspaper, nothing more!"

However, he added, "man is capable of doing such good: let's consider Mother Teresa, for example, a woman of our era." But if "all of us are capable of doing such good" we are "also capable of destroying in great and small measure, in the same family: of destroying the children, not letting the children grow freely, not helping them to grow well" and thus in some way nullifying the children. "We have this capacity, and this is the reason constant meditation, prayer, discussion among ourselves is necessary, to avoid falling into this wickedness that destroys everything."

And "we have the strength" to do it, as "Jesus reminds us," and "today he tells us: Remember. Remember me, who spilled my blood for you. Remember me, who saved you, who saves everyone. Remember me, who has the power to accompany you on the journey of life, not on the road of evil, but on the path of goodness, of doing good for others; not on the path of destruction, but on the path of building—building a family, building a city, building a culture, building a homeland, always more!"

With today's reflection, Francis asked the Lord for the grace to "always choose the right path with his help and not to let ourselves be deceived by the seduction that will lead us down the wrong path" before Lent begins.

STOP AND CHOOSE

Thursday, February 19, 2015
DEUTERONOMY 30:15–20; PSALM 1; LUKE 9:22–25

In the hustle and bustle of life, it is important to have the courage to stop and choose. The season of Lent serves this very purpose. During Mass at St. Martha's on Thursday morning Pope Francis placed emphasis on the need to ask those questions, important for Christian life and to know how to make the right choices.

Interpreting the readings for the day after Ash Wednesday (Deut 30:15–20; Ps 1; Lk 9:22–25), the pontiff explained that "at the beginning of the Lenten journey, the church makes us reflect on the words of Moses and of Jesus: You have to choose." It is thus a reflection on the need we all have, to make choices in life. And Moses, Francis emphasized, "is clear: 'See, I have set before you this day life and good, death and evil': choose." Indeed "the Lord gave us freedom, the freedom to love, to walk on his streets." We are free and we can choose. However, the pope indicated, "it's not easy to choose." It's more comfortable "to live by letting ourselves be carried by the inertia of life, of situations, of habits." This is why "today the church tells us: 'You are responsible; you have to choose.'" And thus the pontiff raised some questions: "Have you chosen? How do you live? What is your lifestyle, your way of living, like? Is it on the side of life or on the side of death?"

Naturally the response should be to "choose the way of the Lord. 'I command you to love the Lord.'" This is how Moses shows us the path of the Lord: "'If your heart turns back and if you do not listen and you let yourself be drawn to prostrate yourself before other gods and serve them, you will perish.' Choose between God and the other gods, those who do not have the power to give us anything, only little things that pass."

Returning to the difficulty of choosing, Francis said he was aware that "we always have this habit of going where the people go, somewhat like everyone." But, he continued, "today the church is telling us: 'stop and choose.' It's good advice. And today," the pope continued, "it will do us good to stop during the day and think: what is my lifestyle like? Which road am I taking?"

After all, in everyday life we tend to take the opposite approach. Many times, he said, "we live in a rush; we are on the run, without noticing what the path is like; and we let ourselves be carried along by the needs, by the necessities of the days, but without thinking." And thus came the invitation to stop: "Begin Lent with small questions that will help one to consider: 'What is my life like?'" The first thing to ask ourselves, the pope explained, is, "Who is God for me? Do I choose the Lord? How is my relationship with Jesus?" And the second: "How is your relationship with your family: with your parents; with your siblings; with your wife; with your husband; with your children?" In fact, these two series of questions are enough, "and we will surely find things that we need to correct."

The pontiff then asked "why we hurry so much in life, without knowing which path we are on." He was explicit about this: "because we want to win, we want to earn, we want to be successful." But Jesus makes us think: "What advantage does a man have who wins the whole world, but loses or destroys himself?" Indeed, "the wrong road," the pope said, is that of always seeking success, one's own riches, without thinking about the Lord, without thinking about family." Returning to the two series of questions on one's relationship with God and with those who are dear to us, the pope emphasized that "one can win everything, yet become a failure in the end. He has failed. That life is a failure." So are those who seem to have had success, those women and men for whom "they've made a monument" or "they've dedicated a portrait," but who didn't "know how to make the right choice between life and death."

And to emphasize the concept, Francis explained that "it will do us good to stop for a bit—five, ten minutes—and ask ourselves the question: what is the speed of my life? Do I reflect on my actions? How is my relationship with God and with my family?" The pope indicated that we can find help in "that really beautiful advice of the psalm: 'Blessed are they who trust in the Lord.'" And "when the Lord gives us this advice—'Stop! Choose today, choose!'—he doesn't leave us on our own; he is with us and wants to help us." And we, for our part, need "only to trust, to have faith in him."

Repeating the words of the psalm, "Blessed are they who trust in the Lord," the pope then urged that we be aware that God does not abandon us. "Today, at the moment in which we stop to think about these things and to make decisions, to choose some-thing, we know that the Lord is with us, is beside us, to help us. He never lets us go alone. He is always with us. Even in the moment of choosing." And he concluded with these instructions: "Let us have faith in this Lord, who is with us, and when he tells us 'choose between good and evil' helps us to choose good." And above all "let us ask him for the grace to be courageous," because "it takes a bit of courage" to "stop and ask myself: how do I stand before God, how are my relationships in the family, what do I need to change, what should I choose?"

Abstaining from Injustice

Friday, February 20, 2015
Isaiah 58:1–9a; Matthew 9:14–15

"Using God to cover up injustice is an extremely grave sin." Pope Francis issued this stern warning against social injustice, most of all the sort caused by those who exploit workers, during Mass on Friday morning in the chapel at St. Martha's House.

The starting point for the pontiff's reflection was the prayer recited at the opening of the Mass, which asked the Lord "to accompany us on this Lenten journey, so that our external observance may correspond to a profound renewal of the Spirit." That is, he clarified, so that "what we do outwardly has a correspondence, bears fruit in the Spirit." In other words, "in order that the outward observance is not a formality."

To render his reflection more concrete, Francis gave the example of one who practices the Lenten fast, thinking, "Today is Friday, I can't eat meat. I'll make myself a nice plate of seafood, a nice banquet . . . I'm observing it, I'm not eating meat." But this way, he added immediately, amounts to "sins of gluttony." This example is "the distinction between formal and real" that is spoken of in the first reading from the book of the prophet Isaiah (58:1–9a). In this passage, the "people lamented because the Lord did not hear their fasts." For his part the Lord reproaches the people, and Pope Francis summarized his words like this: "On the day of your fast, you conduct your business, you torment all your workers. You fast between arguments and quarrels, and hit with wicked fists." Thus, "this is not fasting, not eating meat but then doing all these things: arguing, exploiting the workers," and so on.

Jesus too, Francis added, "condemned this suggestion of piety in the Pharisees, in the doctors of the law: outwardly performing many observances but without truth of heart." The Lord says in fact: "Do not fast anymore as you did today. Change your heart! And what is the fast that I choose? Dissolve the chains of wickedness, cut the thongs of the yoke, let the oppressed go free and break every yoke. Share your bread with the hungry, bring the poor and the homeless into your house, clothe those you see naked, without neglecting your kin." This is "doing justice," the pope said; this "is true fasting, which is not only external, and outward observance, but a fast that comes from the heart."

The pontiff then pointed out that in the Tablets there are "the laws regarding God and the laws regarding one's neighbor," and how they both go together. "I cannot say: 'I fulfill the first three commandments . . . and more or less the others.' No, they are joined: love for God and love for one's neighbor are joined, and if you want to do real, not formal, penance, you must do it before God and also with your brother, with your neighbor." It's enough to consider what the apostle James said: "You can have so much faith, but faith that does no works dies; of what use is it?"

The same is true for "my Christian life," Francis commented. "And those who seek to ease their conscience by attesting, 'I'm a serious Catholic, Father, it's really gratifying . . . I always go to Mass, every Sunday, I take communion . . .'" The pope responded: "Okay. But how is your relationship with your employees? Do you pay them under the table? Do you pay them a fair wage? Do you make contributions for their pension? For their health and social security?" Unfortunately, he continued, so many "men and women have faith, but split the Tablets of the Law: 'Yes, I do this.'—But do you give alms?—'Yes, I always send a check to the church.'—Okay. But at your church, at your home, with those who depend on you, whether they are your children, your grandparents, your employees, are you generous, are you fair?" Indeed, he stated, you cannot "make offerings to the church on the shoulders of injustice" perpetrated against your employees. And that is exactly what the prophet Isaiah sets forth: "One who does not do justice with the people who are dependent on him is not a good Christian." Neither is "one who does not deprive himself of something necessary in order to give it to another who is in need."

Thus "the journey of Lent is twofold: to God and to neighbor." And it must be "real, not merely formal." Francis emphasized that Lent is not only about "not eating meat on Fridays," meaning, "doing some little things" while one's "selfishness, exploitation of others, ignorance of the poor" continue to grow. We need to make a quantum leap, considering especially those who have less. The pontiff explained this by asking each faithful person: "How is your health, you who are a good Christian?—'Good, thank God; but also, when I need to, I immediately go to the hospital and, since I belong to the public health system, they see me right away and give me the necessary medicines.'—It's a good thing, thank the Lord. But tell me, have you thought about those who don't have this relationship with the hospital and when they arrive, they have to wait six, seven, eight hours?" This is not an exaggeration, Francis confided, having heard of a similar experience from a woman who recently waited eight hours for an urgent medical visit.

The pope's thoughts then went to all the "people who live this way here in Rome: children and the elderly who do not have the possibility to be seen by a doctor." And Lent is the season to think about them and how we can help these people. "'But, Father, there are hospitals.' Yes, but you have to wait eight hours and then they have you return a week later." Instead, he indicated, we should be concerned about people in difficulty and ask ourselves: "What are you doing for those people? What will your Lent be like? 'Thank God I have a family who follows the commandments; we don't have problems . . .'—But during Lent is there room in your heart for those who haven't fulfilled the commandments? Who have made mistakes and are in prison? —'Not with those people, no . . .'—But if you are not in prison it is because the Lord has helped you not to fall. Is there room in your heart for inmates? Do you pray for them, that the Lord may help them change their life?"

To conclude, Francis asked the Lord to accompany "our Lenten journey" in order that "our external observance may correspond to a profound renewal of the Spirit."

SHAME AND MERCY

Monday, March 2, 2015
DANIEL 9:4–10; LUKE 6:36–38

Feeling shame and blaming oneself, instead of assigning fault to others, judging and condemning them—this is the first step on the path of Christian life which leads us to ask the Lord for the gift of mercy. The pope suggested this examination of conscience at Mass in the chapel of St. Martha's Guest House on Monday morning.

Francis began his reflection from the day's first reading from the book of Daniel (9:4–10). He explained that the people of God "ask for forgiveness, but not a forgiveness with words: this request for forgiveness is for a forgiveness that comes from the heart because the people feel they are sinners." The people "do not feel they are sinners in theory—because all of us can say 'we are all sinners,' it's true, it's the truth: everyone here!—but before the Lord they tell of the bad things they have done and the good things they have not done." Indeed, the scripture reads: "We have sinned, been wicked and done evil; we have rebelled and departed from your commandments and your laws. We have not obeyed your servants the prophets, who spoke in your name to our kings, our princes, our fathers, and all the people of the land."

In substance, Francis noted, in the words of the people there is a "description of all the evil they have done." Thus, "the people of God, in this moment, blame themselves." They do not criticize "those who persecute us," or their enemies. Instead they look at themselves and say: "I blame myself before you, Lord, and I am ashamed." Such clear words also appear in the passage from Daniel: "O Lord, we are shamefaced."

The pope indicated that this passage "makes us reflect on a Christian virtue, indeed more than one virtue." In fact, "the capacity to blame oneself, self-blame," is "the first step to walking as a Christian." However, "we are all masters, we are all experts" when it comes to "justifying ourselves." We use expressions such as: "It wasn't me; no, it isn't my fault; yes, but not very much . . . That's not how things are . . ."

In short, Francis said, "we all have an alibi" to justify "our shortcomings, our sins." What's more, he added, we so often respond with an "'I don't know!' face," or with an "'I didn't do it; it must have been someone else!' face." In other words, we are always ready to "play innocent." The pope warned, however, that like this, "we don't go forward in the Christian life."

Thus, he reiterated, the capacity for self-blame is "the first step." Surely it is good to do so in confession with a priest. However, Francis asked, "before and after confession, in your life, in your prayer, are you able to blame yourself? Or is it easier to blame others?"

This experience, the bishop of Rome pointed out, gives rise to something a bit odd but which, in the end, gives us peace and health. Indeed, "when we begin to look at what we are capable of, we feel bad, we feel disgust," and we ask ourselves, "Am I capable of doing this?" For example, "when I find envy in my heart and I know this envy is capable of speaking ill of another and morally killing him," I have to ask myself: "Am I capable of it? Yes, I am capable!" This is precisely "how this knowledge begins, this wisdom to blame oneself."

Therefore, Francis said, "if we do not learn this first step of life, we will never make progress on the path of Christian life, of spiritual life." This is because "the first step" is "blaming oneself," even if unsaid and kept between "my conscience and me."

To illustrate, the pope gave a practical example. When we pass by a prison, he said, we might think that the inmates "deserve it." But, he asked, "do you know that were it not for the grace of God, you would be there? Have you thought that you too are capable of doing the things that they did, even worse?" This "is to blame ourselves, not to hide from ourselves the roots of sin that are in us, the many things we are capable of doing, even if they aren't visible."

This attitude, Francis continued, "leads us to feel shame before God, and this is a virtue: shame before God." In order to feel ashamed, we must say, "Look, Lord, I am disgusted with myself, but you are great. To me belongs shame; to you—and I ask for it—mercy." Just as the scripture says: "O Lord, we are shame-faced, for having sinned against you." We can also say, "because we are capable of sinning and of doing so many bad things: But

yours, O Lord, our God, are compassion and forgiveness! Shame
is mine, and mercy and forgiveness are yours." It is a "dialogue
with the Lord" that will "do us good during this Lenten season:
self-blame."

"Let us ask for mercy," the pope said then, referring to the
day's gospel reading from Luke (6:36–38). Jesus "is clear: be
merciful as your Father is merciful." After all, Francis explained,
"when one learns to blame himself he is merciful with others."
And he is able to say: "Who am I to judge him, if I am capable
of doing worse things?" This is an important phrase: "Who am I
to judge another?" This is understood in the light of Jesus' words:
"Be merciful, just as your Father is merciful," and with his call
"not to judge." Instead, the pontiff recognized, "how we like to
judge others, to speak ill of them!" Yet the Lord is clear: "Stop
judging and you will not be judged. Stop condemning and you
will not be condemned. Forgive and you will be forgiven." It is
certainly not an easy road, which "begins with blaming oneself; it
begins from that shame before God and from asking forgiveness
from him: ask forgiveness." Precisely "from that first step we arrive at what the Lord asks us: to be merciful, to judge no one, to
condemn no one, to be generous with others."

From this perspective, the pope prayed that "the Lord, in this
Lenten season, give us the grace to learn to blame ourselves, each
in his solitude," asking ourselves, "Am I capable of doing this?
Am I capable of doing this, with this attitude? With this feeling
that I have inside, am I capable of doing worse things?" He also
invited this prayer: "Have compassion for me, Lord, help me to
feel shame and give me mercy, so that I may be merciful with
others."

WHEN THE LORD EXAGGERATES

Tuesday, March 3, 2015
ISAIAH 1:10, 16–20; MATTHEW 23:1–12

Pope Francis continued his reflections on the theme of conversion, following the Liturgy of the Word. After his call on Monday to blame ourselves, to be truthful with ourselves, and not pretend to be "better than we really are," during Mass at St. Martha's on Tuesday morning the pontiff expanded on "the message of the church" that "today can be summarized in three words: the invitation, the gift, and the pretense." From the book of the prophet Isaiah (1:10, 16–20), the invitation is to conversion: "Give ear to the teaching of our God . . . Wash yourselves; make yourselves clean"! In other words: "Whatever you have inside that isn't good, that which is evil, that which is unclean, must be purified."

In response to the prophet's entreaties: "remove the evil of your doings from before my eyes; cease to do evil, learn to do good," some might say, "but Lord, I don't do evil; I go to Mass every Sunday, I'm a good Christian, I make many offerings." Francis would ask them: "Have you gone into your heart? Are you able to blame yourself for the things you find there?" And when one realizes the need for conversion, one could ask oneself: "How can I convert?" The answer comes from Scripture: "Learn to do good."

"Uncleanliness of heart," the pope said, "is not removed like one removes a stain: we go to the dry cleaner's and come out clean. It is removed by doing." Conversion means "taking a different path, a path other than that of evil." He asked another question: "How do I do good?" The response again comes from the prophet Isaiah: "seek justice, correct oppression; defend the fatherless, plead for the widow." These instructions, Francis explained, were easily understood in Israel, where "the poorest and the neediest were orphans and widows." For each of us this means going to "where the wounds of humanity are, where there is so much pain; and like this, by doing good, you will cleanse your heart, you will be purified! This is the invitation of the Lord."

Conversion means that we are called to do good for "the neediest: the widow, the orphan, the sick, the elderly," those who are "abandoned, whom no one remembers"; but also "the children who cannot go to school" or children "who don't know how to make the sign of the cross." Because, the pontiff pointed out, "in a Catholic city, in a Catholic family there are children who don't know how to pray, who don't know how to make the sign of the cross." Thus it is important "to go to them," to bring "the love of the Lord."

If we do this, the pope asked, "what will the Lord's gift be?" He "will change us," Francis said, referring to what the prophet Isaiah stated: "though your sins are like scarlet, they shall be as white as snow; though they are red like crimson, they shall become like wool." Even in the face of our fear or hesitation—"But Father, I have so many sins! I have committed so very, very many!"—the Lord confirms: "If you take this path, the one to which I invite you, even if your sins are like scarlet, they will become as white as snow."

The pontiff noted, "It's an exaggeration! The Lord exaggerates, but it's the truth," because God, seeing our conversion, "gives us the gift of his forgiveness" and "forgives generously." God does not say: "I'll forgive you up to here, then we'll see the rest . . ." On the contrary, "the Lord always forgives everything, everything." However, Francis emphasized, "if you want to be forgiven" you have to set out on the "path of doing good."

After analyzing the first two words proposed at the start of the homily—first, the "invitation," in other words, setting out on the journey to convert, to do good; and second, the "gift," namely, "I'll give you the greatest forgiveness; I will change you, I will make you completely pure"—the pope moved on to the third word: "presence." Rereading the passage from the gospel according to Matthew (23:1–12) in which Jesus is speaking about the scribes and the Pharisees, Francis indicated that as sinners "we are all clever, and always find a path that isn't the right one, in order to seem more just than we are: it's the path of hypocrisy."

Jesus speaks of this very thing in the passage from the day's liturgy. He "speaks of those men who like to boast about being right: the Pharisees, the doctors of the law, who say the right things, but who do the opposite." These "clever ones," the pontiff explained, find "vanity, pride, power, money" pleasing. They are "hypocrites" because they "pretend to convert, but their heart is false; they are liars." Indeed, "their heart does not belong to the Lord; it belongs to the father of all lies, Satan. And this is the 'pretense' of holiness."

Jesus always spoke very clearly against this attitude. In fact, Jesus preferred sinners "a thousand times" over hypocrites. This, according to Francis, was because at least "sinners told the truth about themselves": "Depart from me, for I am a sinful man, O Lord" (Lk 5:8), as Peter once said. A similar phrase would never fall from the lips of a hypocrite, who would instead say: "I thank you, Lord, that I am not a sinner, that I am just" (cf. Lk 18:11).

Here then are three phrases to meditate upon in this second week of Lent: "the invitation to conversion; the gift that the Lord will give us," which is that of "great forgiveness"; and "the 'trap,' of 'making a pretense' of converting and taking the path of hypocrisy." With these three words at heart we take part in the Eucharist, "our action of grace," in which we hear "the invitation of the Lord: Come to me, eat of me. I will change your life. Do justice, do good, but please, look away from the leaven of the Pharisees, from hypocrisy."

NAMELESS

Thursday, March 5, 2015
JEREMIAH 17:5–10; LUKE 16:19–31

Being worldly means losing your name and having the eyes of your soul "darkened," anesthetized, until you no longer see the people around you. This is the sin that Francis spoke about on Thursday during Mass at St. Martha's.

"Today's Lenten liturgy offers us two stories, two judgments and three names," Francis began. The two stories are those of the parable, narrated by Luke (16:19–31), of the rich man and of the poor man named Lazarus. In particular, the pope stated, the first story is "that of the rich man, who was clothed in purple and the finest linen," who "took good care of himself," and "feasted sumptuously every day." The text, Francis indicated, "doesn't say he was bad," but rather that he had "a comfortable life; he gave himself a good life." In fact, "the gospel doesn't say that he overindulged"; instead his was "a quiet life, with friends." Who knows—perhaps "if he had parents, he surely sent them things so they would have the necessities of life." And maybe "he was a religious man, in his way. Perhaps he recited a few prayers; and surely two or three times a year he went to the temple to make sacrifices and gave large offerings to the priests." And "they, with their clerical cowardliness, thanked him and made him sit in the place of honor." This was the social lifestyle of the rich man presented by Luke.

Then there is "the second story, that of Lazarus," the poor mendicant who lay at the rich man's gate. How is it possible that this man didn't realize that Lazarus was there, below his house, poor and starving? The wounds that the gospel speaks of, the pope said, are "a symbol of the many needs he had." However, "when the rich man left the house, perhaps the car he left in had darkly tinted windows so he couldn't see out." But "surely his soul, the eyes of his soul were tinted dark so he couldn't see." And thus the rich man "saw only his life and didn't realize what was happening" to Lazarus.

In the final analysis, Francis affirmed, "the rich man wasn't bad; he was sick: afflicted with worldliness." And "worldliness transforms souls, makes them lose consciousness of reality; they live in an artificial world," which they create. Worldliness "anesthetizes the soul," and "this is why that worldly man wasn't able to see reality."

This is why, the pope explained, "the second story is clear": there are "so many people who conduct their lives in a difficult way," but "if I have a worldly heart, I will never understand this." After all, "with a worldly heart" it is impossible to comprehend "the necessities and needs of others. With a worldly heart you can go to church, you can pray, you can do many things." But what did Jesus pray for at the Last Supper? "Please, Father, protect these disciples" so that "they do not fall in the world, do not fall into worldliness." And worldliness "is a subtle sin; it's more than a sin: it's a sinful state of soul."

"These are the two stories" presented by the liturgy, the pontiff recapped. "The two judgments," instead, are "a curse and a blessing." The first reading from Jeremiah (17:5–10) reads: "Cursed is the man who trusts in man and makes flesh his arm, whose heart turns away from the Lord." This, Francis stressed, is the profile of the "worldliness we saw" in the rich man. And how will this man end up? Scripture defines him as "'a shrub in the desert, and [he] shall not see any good come. He shall dwell in the parched places of the wilderness'—his soul is a desert—'an uninhabited salt land.'" And all of this "because, in truth, the worldly are alone with their selfishness." Then in the text of Jeremiah there is also a blessing: "Blessed is the man who trusts in the Lord, whose trust is the Lord. He is like a tree planted by water," while the other "was like a shrub in the desert." This, then, is "the final judgment:

nothing is more treacherous for a heart and difficult to heal: that man had a sick heart, so battered by this worldly lifestyle that it was very difficult to heal."

After the two stories and the two judgments, Francis also reiterated "the three names" offered in the gospel reading: "they are that of the poor man, Lazarus, that of Abraham, and that of Moses." Another key to understanding is that the rich man "had no name, because the worldly lose their name," which is merely a feature "of the well-off crowd who need nothing." On the other hand are "Abraham, our father; Lazarus, a man who struggles because he is good and poor and has so much pain; and Moses, the man who gives us the law." But "the worldly have no name. They didn't listen to Moses," because they only need extraordinary manifestations.

In the church, the pontiff continued, "everything is clear. Jesus spoke clearly: this is the way." But "at the end there is a word of consolation: when that unfortunate worldly man, in torment, asks that Lazarus be sent with a bit of water to help him," Abraham, who is the figure of God the Father, responds: "Son, remember . . ." Thus "the worldly have lost their name" and "we too should we have a worldly heart; we have lost our name." However, "we are not orphans. Until the very end, until the final moment, there is the assurance that we have a Father who awaits us. Let us trust in him." And the Father turns to us, calling us "son" and "daughter"—even "in the midst of that worldliness: 'son.'" And this means that "we are not orphans."

In the opening prayer, Francis said, "we asked the Lord for the grace to turn our hearts toward him, who is Father." And thus, the pope concluded, "let us continue the celebration of Mass thinking of these two stories, of these two judgments, of the three names; but above all, of that beautiful word that will always be said until the final moment: 'son.'"

NEVER A SPECTACLE

Monday, March 9, 2015
II KINGS 5:1–15; LUKE 16:19–31

God's way is through "simplicity." There is no point seeking it in some "worldly spectacle." In our life as well, he always acts "in humility, in silence, in the small things." This was Pope Francis' Lenten reflection in his homily during Mass at St. Martha's on Monday morning.

As customary, the pontiff's thoughts were inspired by the Liturgy of the Word, in which the two readings shared "a word in common": "anger, rage." In the day's gospel reading, Luke recounts the episode in which "Jesus returns to Nazareth, goes to the synagogue and begins to speak" (4:24–30). At first "all the people hear him with love"; they are happy, and are astonished by Jesus' words; "they are pleased." But Jesus continues his discourse "and reproaches his people's lack of faith. He recalls that this lack is also historical," and refers to the time of Elisha (in which, the pope recalled, "there were many widows," but God sent the prophet "to a widow from a pagan country"), and to the purification of Naaman the Syrian, in the second book of Kings (5:1–15).

Thus begins the dynamic between the people's expectations and God's response, which was the focus of the pontiff's homily. He explained that, although the people "listened with pleasure to what Jesus was saying," one "was not pleased with what he said" and "some heckler, perhaps, stood up and said, What has this one come to speak to us about? Where did he study, to say these things to us? Make him show us his degree! What university did he attend? This one is the carpenter's son, and we know him well!"

Thus fury and violence break out. The gospel reads that "they put him out of the city, and led him to the brow of the hill" in order to throw him down. However, the pontiff wondered, how did "that admiration, that astonishment" turn into "anger, fury, violence"? This is also what happens to the Syrian general spoken of in the second book of Kings: "This man had faith; he knew the Lord would heal him. But when the prophet says: 'Go and wash,' he is angry." He had other expectations, the pope explained. In fact, he thought Elisha would "'stand, and call on the name of the Lord his God, and wave his hand over the place, and cure the leper . . .' For we have rivers more beautiful than the Jordan." And so he left. Then, however, "his friends reasoned with him," and when he returned, the miracle took place.

The two experiences are far apart in time yet very similar. "What did those people want, those in the synagogue and this Syrian?" Francis asked. On one side, "Jesus reproaches those in the synagogue for their lack of faith." The gospel highlights that "there, in that country, Jesus performed no miracles, due to the lack of faith." On the other, Naaman "had faith, but a particular faith." In any case, Francis emphasized, they were all seeking the same thing: "They wanted a show." But "the way of the good God is not to make a spectacle: God acts in humility, in silence, in the small things." It was no coincidence that "the news of the possible cure" came to the Syrian "from a slave, his wife's servant, a humble young girl." In fact, the pope said, "this is how the Lord moves: through humility. And if we look at the whole of salvation history, we will find that the Lord always works in this way, always, with simple things."

To make this concept better understood, the pontiff made reference to other episodes from scripture. For example, he observed, "the story of creation says nothing of the Lord using a magic wand." He didn't say: "Let us make man," and man was created. But rather, God "worked with mud, simply." And thus, "when he wanted to free his people, he freed them through faith and the trust of one man, Moses." Likewise, "when he wanted to bring down the city of Jericho, he did so through a prostitute." And "also for the conversion of the Samaritans, he requested the work of another sinner."

Actually, the Lord always bewilders man. When "he sent David to fight Goliath, it seemed folly: little David in front of that giant, who had a sword, had many things, and David with only a slingshot and stones." The same happens "when he told the magi that their king was born, the great king." What did they find? "A baby, a manger." Thus, the bishop of Rome repeated, "simple things, the humility of God, this is the divine way, never a spectacle."

After all, he explained, the spectacle was "one of Jesus' three temptations in the desert." In fact, Satan said to him: "Come with me, let's go up to the pinnacle of the temple; throw yourself down and all will see the miracle and will believe in you." The Lord instead reveals himself "in simplicity, in humility."

Thus, Francis concluded, "it will do us good in this Lenten season to think about how the Lord has helped us in our life, about how the Lord has made us go forward, and we will find that he has always done so with simple things." It might always seem to us that everything happens "as if by accident." For "the Lord makes things happen simply. He speaks silently to your heart." Therefore, it will be helpful in this season to remember "the many times" in life in which "the Lord has visited us with his grace" and we have understood that humility and simplicity are his way. This, the pope explained, applies not only in everyday life, but also "in liturgical celebration, in the sacraments," in which "it is beautiful that God's humility is manifest, and not worldly spectacle."

AN OPEN DOOR

Tuesday, March 10, 2015
DANIEL 3:25, 34–43; MATTHEW 18:21–35

"**A**sking forgiveness is not simply making an apology." It isn't easy, just as "it isn't easy to receive God's forgiveness: not because he doesn't want to give it to us, but because we close the door by not forgiving" others. In his homily during Mass at St. Martha's on Tuesday, Pope Francis added an essential element to his reflection on the path of repentance that characterizes Lent: the theme of forgiveness.

His reflection began from the passage of the first reading from the book of the prophet Daniel (3:25, 34–43), which tells of the prophet Azariah, who "is being tested and recalls the trial of his people, who are slaves." But, the pontiff pointed out, the people "weren't slaves by chance; they were enslaved because they abandoned the law of the Lord, because they sinned." Therefore, Azariah prays: "For your name's sake, O Lord, do not deliver us up forever! Do not take away your mercy from us! For we are reduced, we have sinned. We are brought low this day. This day we ask mercy." In other words, Azariah "repents. He asks forgiveness for the sins of his people." Thus, the prophet, put to the test, "does not lament before God." He doesn't say, "You are unjust with us, look at what has happened to us now . . ." Instead, he affirms: "We have sinned and we deserve this." This is the crucial detail: Azariah "has the sense of sin."

The pope then pointed out that Azariah does not say to the Lord: "Sorry, we made a mistake." In fact, "asking forgiveness is something else"; it's not the same as making an apology. These are two different things: the first is simply asking to be excused, the second involves the acknowledgment of having sinned. Indeed, sin "is not simply a mistake. Sin is idolatry," it is worshiping the "many idols that we have: pride, vanity, money, the self, well-being." This is why Azariah doesn't simply apologize, but "begs forgiveness."

The day's passage from the gospel according to Matthew (18:21–35) then led Francis to address the other side of forgiveness: from the forgiveness sought from God to the forgiveness given to our brothers. Peter asks Jesus the question: "Lord, if my brother sins against me, how often must I forgive him?" In the gospel, the pope explained, "there aren't many times in which a person asks forgiveness." He then recalled a few events, such as "the sinner who cries at Jesus' feet, bathes his feet in her tears, and dries them with her hair." In that case, the pontiff said, "that woman had sinned much, loved much, and asked forgiveness." Then he recalled the episode in which Peter, "after the miraculous catch of fish, says to Jesus: 'Stay away from me, for I am a sinner.'" There, however, Peter "realizes that he hadn't made a mistake, that there was something else inside him." And again, we can consider "when Peter cries, the night of Holy Thursday, when Jesus looks at him."

In any case, there are "few moments in which forgiveness is sought." But in the passage from the day's liturgy, Peter asks the Lord how great the measure of our forgiveness must be: "Only seven times?" Jesus answers the apostle "with word play meaning 'always': seventy times seven, that is, you must always forgive."

Here, Francis emphasized, this speaks of "forgiveness," not simply to apologize for a mistake, but to forgive "one who has offended me, who has harmed me, one who through his/her cruelty, has injured my life, my heart."

And thus the question for each of us today is "What is the measure of my forgiveness?" The answer can be found in the parable Jesus tells of the man "who was forgiven" an incredible monetary debt of "many, many millions," and who then, quite happy about being forgiven, goes out and "finds a companion who owes him perhaps a debt of five euros and sends him to jail." The example is obvious: "If I cannot forgive, I cannot ask forgiveness." This is why "Jesus teaches us to pray like this to the Father: 'Forgive us our trespasses as we forgive those who trespass against us.'"

What does this really mean? Pope Francis answered by inventing a dialogue: "Father, I confess, I am going to confess . . .—And what do you do, before confessing?—I think about the things I have done wrong—Okay—Then I ask the Lord's forgiveness and I promise not to do it anymore . . .—Good. And then you go to the priest?" But first "you are missing something: have you forgiven those who have harmed you?" Since the prayer we were taught is "Forgive us our trespasses as we forgive others," we know that "the forgiveness that God will give you" requires "the forgiveness that you give to others."

In conclusion, Francis summarized his meditation. First, "asking forgiveness is not simply making an apology," but "is being aware of the sin, of the idolatry that I have done, of the many idolatries"; second, "God always forgives, always," but he also requires that I forgive, because "if I don't forgive," it is in a sense as if I were closing "God's door." This is a door that we need to keep open: let us allow God's forgiveness to come in so that we may forgive others.

Hearts of Stone

Thursday, March 12, 2015
Jeremiah 7:23–28; Luke 11:14–23

There are no compromises: either we let ourselves be loved "by the mercy of God" or we choose the way "of hypocrisy" and do as we please, allowing our heart to keep growing harder. This is the history of the relationship between God and man, from the time of Abel until now. It was the focus of Pope Francis' homily during Mass at St. Martha's on Thursday morning.

The pontiff began with the words of the Responsorial Psalm—"Harden not your hearts"—and asked: "Why does this happen?" To find the answer, he referred to the first reading from the prophet Jeremiah (7:23–28), which somewhat summarizes the "history of God." But can we really say that "God has a history"? How is this possible, given that "God is eternal"? It's true, Francis explained, "from the moment that God began to dialogue with his people, he entered history."

And the history of God with his people "is a sad history," because "God gave everything" and in exchange "he received only unpleasant things." The Lord said, "Listen to my voice; then I will be your God and you shall be my people. Walk in all the ways that I command you, so that you may prosper." That was the "way" to happiness. "But they obeyed not, nor did they pay heed." Instead, they obstinately continued to walk "in the hardness of their evil hearts." In other words, they did not want to "listen to the word of God."

That choice, the pope explained, has characterized the entire history of the people of God. "Let us consider the assassination, the death of Abel, killed by his brother, the evil heart of envy." Yet, although the people continually "turned their backs" to the Lord, he "never tired." In fact, he "untiringly" sent the prophets. But still, man did not listen. Instead, scripture tells us, "they have stiffened their necks and done worse than their fathers." Thus, "the situation of the people of God worsened through generations."

The Lord says to Jeremiah, "When you speak all these words to them, they will not listen to you, they will not answer. Say to them: This is the nation that does not listen to the voice of the

Lord, or take correction." And then, the pope explained, he adds something "terrible: 'Faithfulness has disappeared.' You are not a faithful people.'" Here, Francis said, it seems that God is weeping: "I have loved you so much, I have given you so much . . ." but you have done "everything against me." A weeping which evokes that of Jesus "looking at Jerusalem." After all, the pontiff explained, "all of this history, in which faithfulness had disappeared, was in Jesus' heart." A history of unfaithfulness regarding "our personal history," because "we do our own will. But in doing so, on the journey of life, we follow a path of hardening: the heart hardens, it turns to stone. The word of the Lord doesn't enter. The people fall away." This is why, the pope indicated, "today, on this Lenten day, we can ask ourselves: do I listen to the voice of the Lord, or do I do what I want, whatever I please?"

The advice of the Responsorial Psalm—"Harden not your hearts"—is found "so many times in the Bible," which, to explain the "unfaithfulness of the people," often uses "the figure of the adulteress." Francis recalled, for example, the well-known passage from Ezekiel 16: "Yours is a long history of adultery. You, the people, have not been faithful to me, you have been an adulterous people." There were also many times in which Jesus "rebukes the disciples for this hardened heart," as he does with those on the road to Emmaus: "O foolish and hardhearted ones!"

The pope explained that the evil heart—of which "we all have a little"—"doesn't allow us to understand God's love. We want to be free," but "with a freedom that enslaves us in the end, rather than that freedom of love that the Lord offers us."

This, the pope highlighted, also happens in institutions. For example, "Jesus heals a person, but the hearts of the doctors of the law, of the priests, of the legal system, are so hard, they are always looking for excuses." And therefore they say to him: "You drive out demons in the name of the demon. You are a demonic sorcerer." The legalists "believe that the life of faith is regulated only by the laws that they make." Jesus called them "hypocrites, whitewashed tombs, outwardly beautiful but inside filled with iniquity and hypocrisy."

Unfortunately, Francis said, the same thing "happened in the history of the church." Let us consider "poor Joan of Arc: today she's a saint! Poor girl: these experts burned her alive because, they said, she was a heretic." Or let's think, more recently, of "Blessed Rosmini: all of his books were on the Index. You couldn't read them; it was a sin to read them. Today he is blessed." In this regard the pontiff underscored that, as "in the history of God with his people, the Lord sent his prophets to tell them that he loved his people"; likewise, "in the church, the Lord sends saints." It is they "who lead forth the life of the church: it is the saints. It isn't the powerful, it isn't the hypocrites." It is the "holy man, the holy woman, the child, the holy youth, the holy priest, the holy sister, the holy bishop . . ." In other words, it is they "whose hearts are not hard," but are instead "always open to the Lord's word of love." It is they who "aren't afraid to let themselves be caressed by the mercy of God. This is why saints are men and women who understand such misery, human misery, and accompany people closely. They do not scorn people."

The Lord is clear with the people who "have lost their faithfulness": "Those who aren't with me are against me." One could ask, "Isn't there a way to compromise, a little here and a little there?" No, the pontiff said. "Either you are on the path of love, or you're on the path of hypocrisy. Either you let yourself be loved by the mercy of God, or you do what you want, according to your heart which grows harder, each time, on this path." There is no "third path of compromise; either you're holy or you take the other path." Whoever "doesn't gather" with the Lord not only "abandons things" but "worse: scatters, destroys. He/she is a corruptor," one "who corrupts."

Because of this unfaithfulness, "Jesus weeps over Jerusalem" and "weeps over each one of us." In Matthew chapter 23, the pope recalled, there is a terrible curse against the "leaders who have hardened hearts and want to harden the hearts of the people." Jesus says: "upon them will come the blood of all the innocent, beginning with that of Abel. They will be held accountable for all the innocent blood shed by their wickedness, by their hypocrisy, by their corrupt, hardened, petrified hearts."

How We Are Changed

Monday, March 16, 2015
Isaiah 65:17–21; John 4:43–54

We are the "dream of God" who, truly in love, wants to "change our life." Through love. He only asks us to have the faith to let him do so. And thus "we can only cry for joy" before a God who "re-creates" us, Pope Francis said on Monday morning during Mass at St. Martha's.

In the first reading, a passage from Isaiah (65:17–21), "the Lord tells us that he creates new heavens and a new earth, that is, he re-creates things," Francis explained, also recalling that "we have spoken many times of these 'two creations' of God: the first, which was done in six days, and the second, when the Lord 're-makes' the world, destroyed by sin, in Jesus Christ." And, the pontiff emphasized, "we have said so many times that this second one is more marvelous than the first." Indeed, he explained, "the first is already a marvelous creation; but the second, in Christ, is even more marvelous."

In his meditation, however, Francis paused "on another aspect," beginning from the passage of Isaiah in which "the Lord speaks about what he is going to make: a new heaven, a new earth." And "we find that the Lord has much enthusiasm: he speaks of joy and says a word: 'I will rejoice in my people.'" Essentially, "the Lord thinks about what he is going to do; he thinks that he, he himself will rejoice with his people." Thus, "it is as if it were a 'dream' of the Lord, as if the Lord 'were dreaming' of us: how beautiful it will be when we are all together, when we are there or when that person, or that one, or another one will walk . . ."

Further clarifying his rationale, Francis returned to "a metaphor that can help us understand. It is as if a young woman with her boyfriend, or a young man with his girlfriend, were to think: 'when we are together, when we get married . . .'" Thus, "God's 'dream': God thinks about each one of us, loves us, dreams of us, dreams of the joy that he will rejoice with us." And this is the very reason that "the Lord wants to 're-create us,' to make our hearts new, to 're-create' our heart in order to make joy triumph."

All this led the pope to ask a few questions: "Have you ever thought, the Lord dreams about me? He thinks about me? I am in the mind, in the heart of the Lord? The Lord is capable of changing my life?" Isaiah also tells us, Francis added, that the Lord "makes many plans: 'We will build houses, plant vineyards, and eat together: all those plans typical of one in love.'"

After all, "the Lord manifests himself enamored of his people," even going so far as to say, "I did not choose you because you are the strongest, the biggest, the most powerful; but I chose you because you are the least of all." Moreover, "it could be said: the poorest of all. I chose you like this, and this is love."

The pope indicated that "this will of the Lord continues, this desire of his to change our life. And we are able to say, if we hear this invitation of the Lord, 'You have changed my mourning into dancing,'" which are "the words that we prayed" in Psalm 29. "I will praise you, Lord, you have rescued me," the psalm also says, thereby acknowledging that the Lord "is capable of changing us, through love; he is in love with us."

"I don't believe any theologian can explain this: it is inexplicable," Francis remarked. Because this is something "we can only reflect on, feel and cry for joy; the Lord can change us." He then asked spontaneously: what do I have to do? The answer is simple: "Believe. Believe that the Lord can change me, that he can." This is exactly what the king's official in Capernaum did, as told in the gospel according to John (4:43–54). That man, whose son was ill, asked Jesus "to come down and heal his son, for he was at the point of death." And Jesus replied to him: "Go; your son will live." Thus, that father "believed the word that Jesus spoke to him and went his way. He believed. He believed that Jesus had the power to heal his child. And he was right."

Faith, Francis explained, "is giving space to this love of God; it is making room for the power, for the power of God, for the power of One who loves me, who is in love with me and who wants this joy with me. This is faith. This is believing: it is making room for the Lord to come and change me."

The pope concluded with a meaningful annotation: "It is curious: this was the second miracle that Jesus performed. And he did it in the same place where he had performed the first, in Cana in Galilee." In today's gospel passage we read, in fact: "So he came again to Cana in Galilee, where he had made the water wine." Again, "in Cana in Galilee, he also changed this boy's death into life." Truly, Francis said, "the Lord can change us, he wants to change us, he loves to change us. And this" he does "through love." And he only asks us for "our faith: in other words, to give space to his love so it may act and bring about a change of life in us."

Don't Close That Door

Tuesday, March 17, 2015
Ezekiel 47:1–9, 12; John 5:1–16

Lent is a propitious time "for each of us and for the whole church" to ask the Lord for "conversion to the mercy of Jesus." Too often, in fact, Christians "are experts at closing the door to people" who, worn down by life and by their mistakes, would instead be ready for a new start, "people whose hearts the Holy Spirit stirs to move forward."

During Mass at St. Martha's on Tuesday, the law of love was at the core of Pope Francis' reflection, which began from the day's Liturgy of the Word. It began with an image: "water that is made fresh." In the first reading, the prophet Ezekiel (47:1–9, 12) talks about water flowing from the temple, "holy water, the water of God, as abundant as the grace of God: ever abundant." The Lord, the pope explained, is indeed generous "in giving his love, in healing our wounds."

Water returns in the gospel according to John (5:1–16), with the image of a pool—"in Hebrew it was called Bethesda"—which had "five porticoes. In these lay a large number of ill, blind, lame, and crippled." In this place there was, in fact, a tradition according to which "from time to time an angel came down" to stir up the waters, and the sick "who jumped in" at that moment "would be healed."

Therefore, the pontiff explained, "there were a lot of people." And that is also why "a man who had been ill for thirty-eight years" was there. He was there, waiting, and Jesus asked him, "Do you want to be well?" The sick man replied, "Sir, I have no one to put me into the pool when the water is stirred up, when the angel comes. While I am on my way, someone else gets down there before me." In other words, Jesus is presented with "a defeated man" who "had lost hope." A sick man, "not just paralyzed," Francis pointed out, but afflicted with "another, much worse disease," sloth.

"Sloth made him sad, lazy," the pope noted. Another person would have "found a way to get there in time, like the blind man in Jericho who shouted and shouted, and they wanted to silence him but he shouted even louder: he found a way." But this man, overcome by thirty-eight years of illness, "didn't want to be healed," didn't have the strength. At the same time, he had a "bitterness of spirit: 'Someone else gets there before me and I am left aside.'" He also had "a little resentment." He was "really a sad soul—defeated, defeated by life."

However, "Jesus has mercy" for this man and says to him, "Rise! Get up, let's put an end to this; take up your mat, and walk!" Francis then described the following scene: "The man was immediately healed and took up his mat and walked, but he was so sick that he couldn't believe it, and perhaps he walked somewhat hesitantly with his mat on his shoulders." At this point other characters come into play: "It is the Sabbath and what does this man find? The doctors of the law," who ask him: "Why are you carrying this? You can't, today is the Sabbath." The man responds, "Well, you know, I've been healed!" Then he adds, "The man who made me well told me: 'take up your mat.'"

Thus a curious thing happened. "The people, instead of rejoicing, of saying: 'How beautiful! Well done!' wonder: 'Who is this man?'" The experts, in other words, begin to investigate and discuss: "Let's see what has happened here, the law . . . We need to defend the law." The man, for his part, continues to walk with his mat, "but a little sadly." The pope commented: "I'm bad, but sometimes I think of what would have happened had this man given a nice check to those doctors. They might have said: 'Go ahead, yes, yes, this time go ahead!'"

Further in the gospel reading, Jesus "finds this man again and says to him: Look, you are well; do not sin anymore, so that nothing worse may happen to you. Go ahead, keep going." And that man goes to the doctors of the law to say: "The person, the man who made me well, is called Jesus. He's the one." We also read that this is why "the Jews began to persecute Jesus because he did this on a Sabbath." Again, Francis said, it was "because he did good even on the Sabbath, and you couldn't do that."

This story, the pope said, bringing his reflection into the present time, it "happens often in life: a man—a woman—who feels sick in spirit, sad, who has made many mistakes in life, at a certain point feels the water stirring." It is "the Holy Spirit who moves something." Or the person "hears a word" and reacts: "I want to go!" Thus "they find courage and go." But "how often today in Christian communities" does that man "find the doors closed." Perhaps he hears: "You cannot, no you cannot; you've made mistakes here and you cannot. If you want to come, come to Mass on Sunday, but stop there, don't do anything more." Thus it happens that "what the Holy Spirit does in people's hearts, Christians destroy with the psychology of the doctors of the law."

The pontiff said he was unhappy about this, because, he emphasized, the church "is Jesus' house and Jesus welcomes, but not only does he welcome: he goes to find people," just as "he went to find" that man. "And if the people are wounded," the pope asked, "what does Jesus do? Does he rebuke them for being wounded? No, he comes and carries them on his shoulders." This, the pope stated, "is called mercy." God speaks of this when "he rebukes his people: 'I desire mercy, not sacrifice.'"

In his usual fashion, the pope ended his reflection with a practical suggestion for daily life: "It is Lent, we must repent." One might say: "Father, there are so many sinners on the street: those who steal, those in the Roma camps . . . ," for example, "and we despise these people." But such a person should be told: "And you? Who are you? Who are you, who close the door of your heart to a man, to a woman who wants to improve, to rejoin the people of God, because the Holy Spirit has stirred his or her heart?" Even today there are Christians who behave like the doctors of the law and "do the same thing they did with Jesus," by objecting: "This one speaks heresy, this one cannot, this one goes against the discipline of the church, this one goes against the law." And thus they close the doors to so many people. He concluded, "Let us ask the Lord today" for "conversion to the mercy of Jesus." Only in this way "will the law be fulfilled, because the law is to love God and neighbor as ourselves."

Three Women and Three Judges

Monday, March 23, 2015
Daniel 13:1–9, 15–17, 19–30, 33–62; John 8:1–11

"Where there is no mercy, there is no justice." Paying the price for this lack of mercy, when faced with "profiteering, depraved, and rigid judges," are the people of God and the church that is "holy, sinful, needy." These were the words of Pope Francis on Monday during Mass at St. Martha's.

Francis immediately pointed out that the day's readings—taken from the book of Daniel (13:1–9, 15–17, 19–30, 33–62) and from the gospel according to John (8:1–11)—"show us two judges of two women." He also mentioned another judgment concerning a woman, "which Jesus recounts in chapter 18 of St. Luke." Thus, "there are three women, and there are three judges: one, an innocent woman, Susanna; another, a sinner, the adulteress; and a third, the one from the gospel of Luke, a poor widow." And "all three, according to some fathers of the church, are allegorical figures of the church: the holy church, the sinful church, and the needy church, for the widow, the orphans were the most needy in that time." This is precisely the reason, the pope explained, that "the fathers thought they were allegorical figures of the church."

However, "the three judges are bad, all three." And, he continued, "I am compelled to emphasize this: in that time a judge was not only a civil judge, he was civil and religious. He was both things together, judging religious and also civil matters." Thus, "all three were corrupt: those who brought the adulteress to Jesus, the scribes, the Pharisees, those who made the law and also passed judgments, they had the corruption of rigidity in their heart." To them, "everything was the letter of the law. What the law said, they felt was pure: the law says this and you must do this . . ." But, Francis remarked, "these were not saints; they were corrupt, corrupt because rigidity of this sort can only go on in a double life." Perhaps they "who condemned these women later went to find them from behind, hidden, to have a good time." And the pope also emphasized that "the rigid ones were—to use the adjective that Jesus gave them—hypocrites: they lived a double life." Such that "those who judge, we think in the church—all three women are allegorical figures of the church—those who judge the church with rigidity have a double life. With rigidity you can't even breathe."

Referring in particular to the passage from the book of Daniel, the pope reemphasized that certainly the two men who unjustly accused Susanna "were not saints either." And Daniel himself, "whom the Holy Spirit moved to prophesy, called them 'old relics of wicked days.'" To one of them he even says: "beauty has deceived you and lust has perverted your heart. This is how you both have been dealing with the daughters of Israel, and they were intimate with you through fear." In other words, those two "were depraved judges; they had the corruption of vice, in this case luxury." And "it is said that when there is this vice of luxury, with years it becomes more savage, more cruel." Thus those two judges "were corrupted by vices."

And "regarding the third judge—the one from the gospel of St. Luke whom I recalled moments ago—Jesus says that he did not fear God and did not take care of anyone; he didn't care, he only cared about himself," Francis said. He was, in short, "a businessman, a judge who in his task of judging did business." And he was thus "corrupt, corrupted by money, by prestige."

The underlying problem, the pope explained, is that these three people—the businessman, the depraved and rigid men— "did not know one word: they did not know what mercy was." Because "corruption took them far from understanding mercy," from "being merciful." However, "the Bible tells us that righteous judgment lies precisely in mercy." And thus "the three women— the saint, the sinner, and the woman in need—suffer from this lack of mercy."

This holds true "even today." And it touches "the people of God" who, "when before these judges, suffer merciless judgment, whether in civil or ecclesiastical" circumstances. After all, the pope clarified, "where there is no mercy, there is no justice." And thus, "when the people of God willingly approach to ask forgiveness, to be judged, how often, how often, they find one of these" judges. They find the "depraved" judges, for example, "who are there, capable of even trying to exploit them," and this "is one of the most serious sins." But unfortunately they also find "the profiteers," to whom "nothing matters and who do not give oxygen to that soul, who do not give hope: it doesn't matter to them." And the people find "the rigid ones, who punish the penitent for what they hide in their own souls." Thus, here are "the holy, sinful, and needy church, and the corrupt judges: be they profiteers, depraved, rigid. This is called a lack of mercy."

In conclusion, Francis recalled "one of the most beautiful words of the gospel, taken right from the day's passage from

John, which really moves me: Has no one condemned you?—No one, Lord—Neither do I condemn you." And this expression of Jesus—"Neither do I condemn you"—is "one of the most beautiful words because it is filled with mercy."

CHRISTIANS? YES, BUT ...

Tuesday, March 24, 2015
NUMBERS 21:4–9; JOHN 8:21–30

How many people say they are Christians but don't accept "the way" that God wants to save us? They are the ones Pope Francis defined as "Christians, yes, but . . . ," incapable of understanding that salvation passes through the cross. And Jesus on the cross—the pontiff explained in his homily during Mass at St. Martha's on Tuesday—is the very "core of the message of the day's Liturgy."

In the passage from the gospel according to John (8:21–30), Jesus says: "When you have lifted up the Son of man . . ." and, foretelling of his death on the cross, evokes the bronze serpent that Moses raised "to heal the Israelites in the desert" and which was recounted in the first reading from the book of Numbers (21:4–9). The people of God enslaved in Egypt, the pope explained, had been freed: "They had truly seen miracles. And when they were afraid, at the time of the Pharaoh's persecution, when they were faced with the Red Sea, they saw the miracle" that God performed for them. The "journey of liberation" thus began in joy. The Israelites "were happy" because they had been "liberated from slavery," happy because "they carried with them the promise of a very good land, a land for them alone," and because "none of them had died" on the first part of the journey. The women were also happy because they had "the jewels of the Egyptian women" with them.

At a certain point, though, the pontiff continued, at the moment in which "the journey was getting long," the people could no longer bear it and "they grew tired." Therefore they began to speak "against God and against Moses: why have you brought us up out of Egypt to die in the wilderness?" They began to "criticize: to speak against God, against Moses," saying, "Here there is no bread and no water, and we loathe this worthless food, this manna." In other words, the Israelites "loathed God's help, a gift of God. And thus that initial joy of liberation became sorrow, lamenting."

They would have probably preferred to be freed by "a magician performing magic with a wand" rather than a God who made them walk and made them "earn salvation" or "at least deserve it in part" by acting "in a certain way."

In the scripture we meet a "discontented people" and, Francis pointed out, "criticizing is a way out of this discontentment." In their discontent, "they vented, but they didn't realize that the soul becomes poisoned with this attitude." Thus, the serpents arrive, because "like this, like the venom of serpents, at this moment these people had a poisoned spirit."

Jesus, too, speaks of the same attitude, of "this way of not being content, not satisfied." The pontiff then referred to a passage from the gospels of both Matthew (11:17) and Luke (7:32): "When Jesus speaks of this attitude he says: 'How are you to be understood? Are you like those youths in the square: we played for you and you did not dance; we wailed and you did not mourn. Does nothing satisfy you?'" The problem "wasn't salvation" but rather "liberation," because "everyone wanted this"; the problem was "God's way: they didn't like dancing to God's song; they didn't like mourning to God's lamentations." So "what did they want?" They wanted, the pope explained, to act "according to their own thoughts, to choose their own path to salvation." But that path "didn't lead anywhere."

This is an attitude that we still encounter today. "Among Christians," Francis asked, how many are "somewhat poisoned" by this discontentment? We hear, "Yes, truly, God is good. Christians, yes, but . . ." They are the ones, he continued, "who end up not opening their hearts to God's salvation" and who "always ask for conditions"; the ones who say, "Yes, yes, yes, I want to be saved," but on the path of their own choosing. This is how "the heart becomes poisoned." This is the heart of "lukewarm Christians" who always have something to complain about: "'Why has the Lord done this to me?'—'But he saved you, he opened the door for you, he forgave you of so many sins'—'Yes, yes, it's true, but . . .'" Thus the Israelites in the desert said: "I would like water, bread, but the kind I like, not this worthless food. I loathe it." And we too "so often say that we loathe the divine way."

Francis emphasized: "Not accepting the gift of God in his way, that is the sin; that is the venom; that poisons the soul; it takes away your joy, it doesn't let you go."

So "how does the Lord resolve this? With the poison itself, with sin itself." In other words, "He takes the poison, the sin, upon himself and is lifted up." Thus "this warmth of soul, this being halfway Christians," this being "Christians, yes, but . . ." becomes healed. The healing, the pope explained, comes only by "looking to the cross," by looking to God who takes on our sins: "my sin is there." However, "how many Christians in the desert die of their sorrow, of their lamenting, of their not wanting God's way." This is for every Christian to reflect upon: while God "saves us and shows us what salvation is like," I "am not really able to tolerate a path that I don't like much." This is the "selfishness that Jesus rebukes in his generation," which said of John the Baptist: "He has a demon." And when the Son of Man came, he was defined as a "glutton" and a "drunkard." And so, the pope asked, "who understands you?" He added, "I too, with my spiritual caprice regarding the salvation that God gives me, who understands me?"

Therefore, there is an invitation to the faithful: "Look at the serpent, the venom there in the Body of Christ, the poison of all the sins of the world, and ask for the grace to accept the divine way of salvation; to also accept this food, so wretched that the Hebrews complained about it": the grace, that is, "to accept the ways by which the Lord leads me forth." Francis concluded by praying that Holy Week may "help us to leave behind this temptation to become 'Christians, yes, but . . .'"

Ode to Joy

Thursday, March 26, 2015
Genesis 17:3–9; John 8:51–59

Joy and hope are Christian traits. It is sad to find a believer who knows no joy and is fearful in his attachment to cold doctrine. This was the inspiration for Francis' ode to joy during Thursday's Mass at St. Martha's.

At the beginning of Mass, the pope acknowledged the Carmelite "Hour of Prayer for Peace." "Dear brothers and sisters," he said, "the day after tomorrow, March 28, will be the fifth centenary of the birth of St. Teresa of Jesus, Virgin Doctor of the church." And "on that day, at the request of the superior general of the Discalced Carmelites, who is here today with Fr. Vicari, all the Carmelite communities in the world will hold an hour of prayer for peace. I wholeheartedly join this initiative," Francis affirmed, "in order that the flame of God's love may extinguish the fires of war and of violence that plague mankind, and that dialogue may prevail over armed conflict everywhere." He concluded these initial remarks by asking: "May St. Teresa of Jesus intercede for this, our petition."

The pope's homily began with a reference to "two readings offered by today's liturgy" (Gen 17:3–9 and Jn 8:51–59), which "speak of time, of eternity, of years, of the future, of the past." In fact, "time seems to be very important in the liturgical message" of the day, he said. However, Francis chose to reflect on different words that he believed, he said, "to really be the message in the church today." They are the words of Jesus as narrated by John the evangelist: "Your father Abraham rejoiced that he was to see my day; he saw it and was glad."

Thus, today's central message is "the joy of hope, the joy of trusting in God's promise, the joy of fruitfulness." In fact, "Abraham, in the time that the first reading speaks about, was ninety-nine years old and the Lord appeared to him and secured the covenant" with these words: "Behold, my covenant is with you, and you shall be a father."

Abraham, Francis continued, "had a twelve- or thirteen-year-old son: Ishmael." But God assured him that he would become "the father of a multitude of nations" and "changed his name." Then "he continued and asked him to be faithful to the covenant," saying: "I will establish my covenant between me and you and your descendants after you throughout their generations for an everlasting covenant." Essentially, God told Abraham: "I give you everything, I give you time; I give you all, you will be father."

Surely, said the pope, Abraham "was happy about this, was filled with comfort" in hearing the Lord's promise: "Within a year you shall have another son." Of course, in hearing these words, Abraham laughed, the Bible says afterwards: "how, a son at one hundred years old?" Yes, "he had begotten Ishmael at eighty-seven years, but at one hundred years a son is too much. It was incomprehensible!" Therefore, "he laughed." But "that smile, that laughter was the beginning of Abraham's joy." Here then, the pope brought back the essence of Jesus' words as the day's central message: "Your father Abraham rejoiced." Indeed, he "didn't dare believe and said to the Lord: 'But if only Ishmael should live in your presence.'" To which he received the response, "No, it shall not be Ishmael. It shall be another."

Thus, the pope stated, Abraham "was joyful" and "a little later his wife Sarah also laughed. She was hiding behind the tent door, listening to what the men were saying." And "when these messengers of God gave Abraham the news about his son, she too laughed." And this really was "the beginning of the great joy of Abraham," Francis said. Yes, "the great joy: he rejoiced in the hope of seeing this day; he saw it and was filled with joy." The pope recommended that we look to "this beautiful icon: Abraham who was before God, who bowed himself to the earth. He heard this promise and his heart opened to hope and was filled with joy."

This is precisely "what these doctors of the law did not understand," Francis said. "They did not understand the joy of the promise; they didn't understand the joy of hope; they didn't understand the joy of the covenant. They did not understand." And "they didn't know how to rejoice, for they had lost the sense of joy that only comes from faith." However, the pope explained, "our father Abraham was able to rejoice because he had faith; he had been made righteous in faith." Meanwhile the doctors of the law "had lost the faith; they were doctors of the law, but without faith!" Moreover: "they had lost the law! Because the center of law is love, love for God and for neighbor." However, they "had only a system of specific teachings that they refined further every day so that no one would touch them."

They were "men without faith, without laws, attached to doctrines that had even become a casuistic approach." Francis also proposed practical examples: "We can pay taxes to Caesar, can't we? This woman, who was married seven times, when she went to heaven would she be the spouse of those seven?" And "this casuistry was their world: an abstract world, a world without love, a world without faith, a world without hope, a world without trust, a world without God." For this very reason "they were unable to rejoice." They didn't even enjoy themselves at parties, the pope affirmed, although they surely "uncorked a few bottles when Jesus was condemned." But they were always "without joy," or moreover, "afraid that one of them, perhaps while drinking," would remember the promise that "he would rise." And thus, "straightaway, with fear, they went to the prosecutor to say 'please, be careful with this one, that it isn't a trick.'" All this was because "they were afraid."

But "this is life without faith in God, without trust in God, without hope in God," the pope affirmed once again. The life of these men, he added, "who only when they understood that they had been wrong" did they think that the only choice left was to take up stones to throw at Jesus. "Their heart had become stone." Indeed "it is sad to be a believer without joy," Francis explained, "and there is no joy when there is no faith, when there is no hope, when there is no law, but only the prescriptions, the cold doctrine. This is what counts." In contrast, the pope again proposed "Abraham's joy, that beautiful act of Abraham's laughter" when he heard the promise of having "a son at one hundred years," as well as "Sarah's smile, a smile of hope." This is because "the joy of faith, the joy of the gospel is the touchstone of a person's faith: without joy that person is not a true believer."

In conclusion, Francis used the very words of Jesus: "Your father Abraham rejoiced that he was glad to see my day; he saw it and was glad." The pope then asked "the Lord for the grace to rejoice in hope, the grace to be able to see the day of Jesus when we will be with him, and the grace of joy."

Scripture Index

OLD TESTAMENT